Moving to France: A Comprehensive Guide to Relocating and Settling in the Land of Elegance and Culture by Anthony Russo

This book was published in 2023 by Mamba Press

CW01507284

Table of Contents

Chapter 1: Planning Your Move

Chapter 2: Legal and Administrative Procedures

Chapter 3: Finding Accommodation

Chapter 4: Education and Healthcare

Chapter 5: Employment and Entrepreneurship

Chapter 6: Learning the Language and Adapting to the Culture

Chapter 7: Transportation and Getting Around

Chapter 8: Making Friends and Building a Social Life

Chapter 9: Exploring French Culture and Leisure Activities

Chapter 10: Overcoming Challenges and Celebrating Success

Appendix: Useful Resources and Contacts

MOVING TO FRANCE

A COMPREHENSIVE GUIDE TO RELOCATING AND
SETTLING IN THE LAND OF ELEGANCE AND CULTURE

BY ANTHONY RUSSO

2023

Chapter 1: Planning Your Move

Moving to a new country is a significant life decision that requires careful planning and preparation. In this chapter, we will explore the essential steps to take when considering relocating to France. From understanding your motivations for the move to researching potential destinations, this chapter sets the foundation for a successful and smooth transition.

Section 1: Deciding to Move

- Reflecting on Your Reasons: Evaluate the factors driving your decision to move to France, such as career opportunities, lifestyle change, education, or personal growth.

- Discussing the Move with Family: Involve your family members in the decision-making process, considering their needs and concerns.

Section 2: Understanding Visa and Residence Permit Requirements

- Visa Categories: Learn about the different visa types available for long-term stays in France, including work visas, student visas, and family reunion visas.

- Residence Permits: Explore the process of obtaining a residence permit and the conditions for its renewal or conversion to long-term residency.

Section 3: Researching French Cities and Regions: Finding Your Ideal Destination

- Regional Diversity: Discover the unique characteristics and offerings of various French regions and cities, from the bustling streets of Paris to the tranquil countryside of Provence.

- Factors to Consider: Assess factors like job opportunities, cost of living, climate, culture, and proximity to amenities when choosing your future home.

Section 4: Setting a Budget: Cost of Living and Financial Planning

- Cost of Living Estimates: Understand the average expenses in France, including accommodation, transportation, food, utilities, and healthcare.

- Financial Planning: Develop a budget that accounts for both initial moving costs and ongoing living expenses.

Section 5: Navigating Language and Cultural Barriers

- French Language Basics: Familiarize yourself with essential French phrases and expressions to facilitate communication during your initial stay.

- Cultural Awareness: Learn about French customs, traditions, and social etiquette to integrate smoothly into the local culture.

By the end of this chapter, you will have gained valuable insights into your motivations for moving, be aware of the necessary legal procedures, have a clearer picture of potential destinations in France, and have started preparing your budget and language skills. Moving to France is an exciting adventure, and with careful planning, you can ensure a successful and enriching experience in your new home.

1. Deciding to Move

Deciding to move to a new country is a momentous decision that requires comprehensive contemplation and assessment of various aspects of your life. Relocating to France, a country renowned for its rich history, cultural diversity, and breathtaking landscapes, presents an enticing opportunity for new experiences and personal growth. Before embarking on this life-changing journey, it is essential to delve into the core reasons driving your desire to move and evaluate the impact it will have on your personal and professional life.

First and foremost, take the time for self-reflection to understand your motivations and objectives for moving to France. Whether it's the allure of a different lifestyle, career advancement, educational opportunities, or simply the allure of exploring a new culture, identifying the underlying reasons will provide clarity and focus as you consider this significant change.

Researching and understanding French culture and lifestyle is pivotal in making an informed decision. Familiarize yourself with the social customs, traditions, and language to assess your readiness and adaptability to embrace a new way of life. Language proficiency, particularly in French, plays a critical role in your integration into society and daily interactions, making language learning a valuable asset as you plan your move.

Evaluate the career and educational opportunities available in France to ensure that the move aligns with your long-term aspirations. Research the job market in your field of expertise and identify potential employment prospects and growth avenues. If you plan to study in France or have children who will attend school, exploring educational institutions, courses, and qualifications becomes crucial in shaping your decision.

Financial preparedness is a fundamental consideration when contemplating a move to France. Research the cost of living in different regions, factoring in expenses such as housing, transportation, food, utilities, and healthcare. Assess your current financial stability to determine if you have the necessary resources to support yourself and your family during the initial stages of relocation.

Family considerations are pivotal in the decision-making process. Involve your family members in discussions about the move, considering their preferences, concerns, and potential adjustments to a new environment. For families with children, exploring the availability and quality of educational institutions and childcare options becomes paramount.

Understand the legal and administrative preparations required for moving to France. Familiarize yourself with visa and residence permit options based on the purpose and duration of your stay. Ensure all essential documents, such as passports, birth certificates, marriage certificates, and academic qualifications, are in order and easily accessible.

Embracing change and challenges is essential in preparing for a move to a new country. Assess your adaptability to different environments, cultural differences, and potential language barriers. Being open to embracing change and adjusting to a different way of life will facilitate a smoother transition.

Weigh the prospective benefits and potential challenges of moving to France. Create a comprehensive list that outlines the advantages, such as career opportunities, cultural experiences, and personal growth, alongside the possible drawbacks, including homesickness and cultural adjustments.

Seek guidance and support throughout the decision-making process. Reach out to friends, colleagues, or expatriates who have experience living in France to learn from their insights and experiences. Consider consulting immigration experts or relocation services to guide you through the process and address any legal or administrative complexities.

Ultimately, trust your instincts and intuition when making this life-altering decision. By thoroughly examining these aspects and conducting extensive research, you can make an informed and confident choice about moving to France. Remember that moving to a new country is a unique and personal experience, and taking the time to assess your motivations and readiness will pave the way for a successful and fulfilling journey in the enchanting land of France.

2. Understanding Visa and Residence Permit Requirements

Understanding the visa and residence permit requirements is a crucial step in the process of moving to France. As a non-EU/EEA citizen, obtaining the appropriate visa and residence permit is necessary for a long-term stay in the country. In this section, we will delve into the various visa categories and the essential steps involved in securing a residence permit, ensuring a smooth and legal transition to your new life in France.

France offers different visa categories to cater to various purposes of stay. The Short-Stay Schengen Visa allows for visits of up to 90 days within a 180-day period for tourism, business, or family visits. For longer stays, there are specific long-stay visa options, such as the French Work Visa for skilled workers, the Student Visa for pursuing education, and the Family Reunion Visa for joining family members already residing in France.

Applying for a visa requires careful preparation and adherence to specific procedures. Compile all the necessary documents, including proof of accommodation, financial means, travel insurance, and the purpose of your stay. Once you have gathered the required paperwork, schedule an appointment at the French consulate or embassy in your home country to submit your visa application. Be mindful of the processing time, which may vary depending on the type of visa and the volume of applications.

For a long-term stay beyond the validity of your visa, a residence permit becomes essential. Various types of residence permits are available, such as the "VLS-TS" for temporary stays and the "Carte de Séjour" for long-term residency. Each permit has its validity period and requirements for renewal or conversion to a different type of permit.

Upon arrival in France, you will need to complete certain administrative procedures. Registering with the local authorities through the Office Français de l'Immigration et de l'Intégration (OFII) is mandatory for certain visa categories. Additionally, you may be required to undergo a medical examination as part of the OFII process.

To ensure a smooth and legal transition, make sure to comply with French immigration laws. Abide by the conditions specified in your visa and residence permit, including the duration of your stay and any work or study restrictions. Overstaying your visa can result in penalties and legal complications.

In conclusion, understanding the visa and residence permit requirements is vital when considering a move to France. Familiarize yourself with the various visa categories, compile the necessary documents, and follow the application procedures diligently. Be prepared for the administrative processes upon arrival and ensure compliance with French immigration laws to avoid any legal issues. By securing the appropriate visa and residence permit, you can embark on your journey to France with confidence and peace of mind, ready to embrace the new experiences and opportunities that await you in this captivating country.

3. Researching French Cities and Regions: Finding Your Ideal Destination

France offers a plethora of cities and regions, each with its unique charm, culture, and lifestyle. Conducting comprehensive research is essential in finding the ideal destination that aligns with your preferences and needs. Start by identifying your priorities and the kind of environment that suits your desired lifestyle. Whether you crave the vibrant energy of a bustling city, the tranquility of the countryside, or the coastal allure, France has something to offer for everyone.

Explore the popular French cities to gain insights into their distinct characteristics. Paris, the capital city, boasts a rich history, world-renowned cultural landmarks, and a diverse blend of neighborhoods, making it a popular choice for many. Lyon, the gastronomic capital, offers a vibrant cultural scene and a strong sense of community. Marseille, on the Mediterranean coast, captivates with its maritime ambiance and multicultural influences. Bordeaux, known for its wine and elegant architecture, appeals to those seeking a refined yet relaxed lifestyle.

The French countryside, too, presents a plethora of enchanting regions to consider. Provence, with its lavender fields and picturesque villages, offers a laid-back lifestyle and a deep appreciation for nature's beauty. Brittany, in northwest France, boasts rugged coastlines, Celtic heritage, and a maritime spirit. Alsace, near the German border, enchants with its fairytale-like towns, vineyards, and a blend of French and German influences.

Practical considerations are essential when researching French cities and regions. If you plan to work or study, evaluate the job market and educational opportunities in your potential destinations. Compare the cost of living, including housing, transportation, and everyday expenses, to ensure it aligns with your budget.

Climate and geography are significant factors to consider. France experiences varied climates across different regions. The Mediterranean coast offers mild winters and hot summers, while the Alpine regions provide winter sports enthusiasts with ample opportunities. The Atlantic coast provides temperate weather and stunning beaches for relaxation.

Embrace the local culture and activities by researching the cultural attractions and leisure opportunities available in your chosen destination. Consider the availability of outdoor activities like hiking, biking, or water sports if you enjoy an active lifestyle.

Seeking out expat communities and online resources can be invaluable in gaining firsthand experiences and insights. Engage with expatriates who have already settled in your potential destination to learn about the expat experience, local tips, and challenges they may have encountered.

In conclusion, thorough research is the key to finding your ideal destination in France. Identify your lifestyle priorities and preferences, explore the cities and regions that resonate with your aspirations, and consider practical aspects like job opportunities and cost of living. Embrace the unique cultural experiences and activities each destination offers. Engage with expat communities and online resources to gain valuable insights. By taking the time to research and find the perfect fit, you can ensure a seamless and fulfilling transition to your chosen destination in the enchanting country of France.

4. Setting a Budget: Cost of Living and Financial Planning

When considering a move to France, setting a realistic budget is a crucial step in ensuring a smooth and comfortable transition. Understanding the cost of living and engaging in comprehensive financial planning will help you make informed decisions and avoid financial challenges in your new life abroad.

Researching the cost of living in different regions of France is essential. Cities like Paris and Lyon generally have a higher cost of living due to their popularity and urban amenities. In contrast, smaller towns and rural areas often offer a more affordable lifestyle. Consider factors such as housing costs, transportation expenses, food prices, utilities, healthcare, and leisure activities when estimating your budget.

Housing is typically one of the most significant expenses for expatriates. Rent prices in major cities can be relatively high, especially in prime neighborhoods. It is essential to research different housing options, such as apartments, houses, and shared accommodations, to find a balance between affordability and location convenience.

Transportation costs can vary depending on your chosen location and daily commuting needs. Cities often have well-developed public transportation systems, offering cost-effective ways to get around. In more rural areas, owning a car might be necessary, so consider expenses like insurance, fuel, and maintenance.

Food expenses should also be factored into your budget. France is renowned for its culinary delights, and dining out can be a significant part of the experience. However, cooking at home can be a more economical option, especially if you embrace local markets and fresh produce.

Healthcare is a critical consideration for your financial planning. France has an excellent healthcare system, but it's essential to understand how it works and consider obtaining health insurance to cover any potential medical expenses.

Financial planning should encompass not just your immediate expenses but also your long-term financial stability. Evaluate your savings, assets, and potential sources of income while in France. If you plan to work, research the job market and assess potential earnings.

Before moving, create a detailed budget that accounts for all your projected expenses. Be conservative in your estimates to account for unforeseen costs. Allow some flexibility in your budget to accommodate unexpected expenses and emergencies.

Consider consulting with financial experts or expatriate financial advisors who can provide guidance specific to your situation. They can help you navigate taxation matters, retirement planning, and investment options while living in France.

By setting a well-researched and comprehensive budget, you can embark on your journey to France with financial confidence. A clear understanding of the cost of living and thoughtful financial planning will help you make informed choices, ensuring that your time in France is financially stable and enjoyable. Embrace the opportunity to immerse yourself in the vibrant French culture while having peace of mind about your financial well-being.

5. Navigating Language and Cultural Barriers

Moving to a new country brings with it the challenge of adapting to a different language and culture. For those relocating to France, navigating language and cultural barriers is an integral part of successfully integrating into society and fostering meaningful connections with the local community.

Language is a fundamental aspect of communication, and in France, French is the official language. While English is widely understood, especially in major cities and tourist areas, learning and using French will significantly enhance your experience and interactions with locals. Consider enrolling in language classes before moving or attending language courses upon arrival. Immersing yourself in the language through daily practice, conversing with locals, and watching French media can help you build fluency and confidence.

Cultural awareness is equally important in adapting to life in France. Understanding French customs, social norms, and etiquettes will help you navigate social interactions and demonstrate respect for local traditions. For example, the French value politeness and formality in greetings, so learning basic phrases like "bonjour" (hello) and "merci" (thank you) can go a long way in making a positive impression.

One of the cultural cornerstones in France is its gastronomy. Embrace the French love for food and dining by experiencing local cuisine and dining customs. Participating in social gatherings and local events will provide valuable insights into the French way of life and create opportunities to build connections with people.

Integrating into a new culture can be challenging, but being open-minded and receptive to new experiences is key. Engaging in local activities, joining clubs or organizations, and volunteering can help you meet new people and build a support network. Additionally, seeking out expatriate communities can provide a sense of familiarity and a space to share experiences and tips.

Patience and a sense of humor are essential when facing language and cultural barriers. Embrace mistakes as opportunities for growth and learning. The French appreciate effort and will likely be understanding and supportive of your attempts to communicate in their language.

Remember that adapting to a new culture is a gradual process. Be kind to yourself and allow time to acclimate to your new surroundings.

As you become more familiar with the language and customs, you will feel more at ease in your daily interactions and experience a deeper connection with the vibrant French culture.

In conclusion, navigating language and cultural barriers is a vital aspect of successfully integrating into French society. Embrace the opportunity to learn and speak French, as it will enrich your experience and facilitate meaningful connections with locals. Embrace the French way of life, participate in local customs, and show respect for their culture. By being open-minded, patient, and embracing the beauty of cultural diversity, you will embark on a fulfilling journey in the enchanting and welcoming country of France.

Chapter 2: Legal and Administrative Procedures

Moving to a new country involves a series of legal and administrative procedures to ensure a smooth and lawful transition. France has specific requirements and processes for expatriates, making it essential to familiarize yourself with the necessary steps to comply with immigration laws and regulations. In this chapter, we will guide you through the legal and administrative procedures involved in moving to France and provide valuable insights to help you navigate the system effectively.

Section 1: Visa and Residence Permits

- Understanding Visa Categories: Explore the different visa categories available for non-EU/EEA citizens, including short-stay Schengen visas, long-stay visas for work, study, family reunification, and other purposes.

- Visa Application Process: Learn about the documents required for visa applications, the submission process, and the expected waiting time for visa approval.

- Residence Permit Requirements: Understand the various types of residence permits and the conditions for obtaining and renewing them based on the purpose and duration of your stay in France.

- Addressing Family Reunification: If you plan to be joined by family members, explore the specific procedures and documents necessary for family reunification in France.

Section 2: Registration and Integration

- OFII Process: Learn about the Office Français de l'Immigration et de l'Intégration (OFII) and its role in the integration process, including the mandatory medical examination and procedures for obtaining the OFII stamp on your passport.

- Integration Contract: Explore the Integration Contract, an important aspect of the immigration process for certain visa and residence permit categories, and understand its requirements and benefits.

- Registering with Local Authorities: Know the procedure for registering your arrival with the local town hall (mairie) and obtaining a "Certificat d'Enregistrement" if you plan to stay in France for more than three months.

Section 3: Health Insurance and Social Security

- French Healthcare System: Gain an overview of the French healthcare system, including public and private healthcare options, and understand how to access medical services as an expatriate.

- Health Insurance Coverage: Learn about the different health insurance options available to expatriates in France, including private health insurance and the French national health insurance system (CPAM).

- Social Security Contributions: Understand the requirements and obligations for contributing to the French social security system, depending on your employment status and income.

Section 4: Taxation and Financial Obligations

- French Tax System: Familiarize yourself with the French tax system and its implications for expatriates, including income tax, property tax, and wealth tax.

- Tax Residency: Determine your tax residency status and understand the criteria that determine whether you are considered a tax resident in France.

- Tax Filing and Reporting: Learn about the process of filing tax returns in France, including deadlines and required documentation.

Section 5: Driving and Transportation

- International Driving Permits: If you plan to drive in France, understand the requirements for obtaining and using an international driving permit.

- Registering and Insuring Your Vehicle: Learn about the process of registering and insuring your vehicle in France, including the necessary paperwork and insurance options.

By delving into these legal and administrative procedures, you can proactively prepare for your move to France and ensure compliance with the country's regulations. Each section will provide detailed insights and step-by-step guidance, empowering you to confidently navigate the legal aspects of your relocation and focus on embracing the cultural richness and opportunities that await you in your new home.

1. Visa and Residence Permits

Navigating the visa and residence permit process is one of the most crucial aspects of moving to France as a non-EU/EEA citizen. Understanding the various visa categories and residence permit requirements is essential to ensure a legal and smooth transition. The first step is identifying the appropriate visa category based on the purpose of your stay. For short-term visits of up to 90 days within a 180-day period, the Schengen visa is suitable for tourism, business, or family visits. However, for longer stays, such as work, study, family reunification, or other purposes, obtaining a long-stay visa is necessary.

The visa application process requires careful preparation and attention to detail. You must gather all the necessary documents, which may include proof of accommodation, financial means, travel insurance, and the purpose of your stay. It is essential to apply for the visa at the French consulate or embassy in your home country and schedule an appointment well in advance. The processing time for visa applications can vary, so early planning is critical to avoid delays in your travel arrangements.

Once you arrive in France, you may need to obtain a residence permit if you plan to stay beyond the validity of your visa. There are different types of residence permits, each with specific requirements and conditions. For temporary stays, the "VLS-TS" permit is suitable, while the "Carte de Séjour" is relevant for long-term residency. Understanding the validity and renewal process of each permit is crucial to ensure a continuous legal stay in France.

For individuals planning to be joined by family members, the family reunification process requires additional documentation and procedures. It is essential to be well-informed about the requirements for bringing family members to France and prepare the necessary paperwork in advance.

Registering with the local authorities is a mandatory step in the immigration process. The Office Français de l'Immigration et de l'Intégration (OFII) plays a vital role in the integration process. Certain visa holders are required to undergo a medical examination and obtain an OFII stamp on their passport upon arrival. Additionally, an Integration Contract may be necessary for specific visa and residence permit categories, outlining the efforts and commitments expected from newcomers to integrate into French society successfully.

Compliance with French immigration laws is essential throughout your stay. Understanding the terms and conditions of your visa and residence permit is crucial to avoid legal issues. Overstaying your visa or violating the terms of your permit can lead to penalties, potential deportation, or difficulty obtaining future visas.

In conclusion, Section 1 of this guide provides comprehensive insights into the visa and residence permit process for moving to France. Understanding the different visa categories, preparing necessary documents, and adhering to application procedures are essential steps to ensure a smooth transition. Registering with the local authorities and complying with immigration laws will help you begin your life in France legally and confidently. By carefully following the guidelines presented in this section, you can focus on embracing the cultural richness and opportunities that await you in this captivating country.

2. Registration and Integration

Registering with the local authorities and ensuring a smooth integration process are critical steps for expatriates moving to France. Upon arrival, certain administrative procedures must be followed to comply with the country's immigration laws and foster a sense of belonging within the local community.

One of the primary tasks is registering with the local town hall (mairie) if you plan to stay in France for more than three months. This process involves obtaining a "Certificat d'Enregistrement," which serves as proof of your legal residence in the country. The certificate may be required for various purposes, such as opening a bank account, enrolling in schools, or accessing healthcare services. It is essential to complete this registration promptly to avoid any legal complications during your stay.

The Office Français de l'Immigration et de l'Intégration (OFII) plays a crucial role in the integration process for certain visa holders. Upon arrival, individuals with specific visa categories must contact the OFII to complete the mandatory integration process. This includes attending a medical examination and fulfilling certain obligations outlined in the Integration Contract. The Integration Contract emphasizes the importance of learning the French language, understanding French values and customs, and engaging in civic responsibilities. Compliance with the Integration Contract is vital for successful integration and may impact future residency rights.

For individuals planning to work or study in France, certain work and study permits may require additional registration with specific authorities. For example, students may need to register at the Caisse d'Allocations Familiales (CAF) to apply for housing assistance or other benefits.

Integration into French society extends beyond legal procedures and involves embracing the local culture and community. Engaging in social activities, participating in local events, and immersing yourself in

French customs are excellent ways to connect with the community and build meaningful relationships.

Joining clubs, organizations, or volunteering can also be instrumental in meeting new people and building a support network. Engaging with expatriate communities can provide a sense of familiarity and camaraderie while also facilitating the sharing of experiences and tips.

Adapting to a new culture can be a gradual process, and patience is essential during this period of adjustment. Embrace the opportunity to learn from and interact with people from diverse backgrounds, and be open to making new friends. Remember that integrating into a new society involves both giving and receiving, so be willing to share your own culture and experiences with others as well.

In conclusion, Section 2 of this guide emphasizes the importance of registration and integration for expatriates moving to France. Registering with the local authorities and complying with immigration requirements are crucial for a legal and secure stay. Engaging in the integration process, including the OFII procedures and fulfilling the Integration Contract obligations, is essential for successfully acclimating to the French way of life. Embrace the opportunity to immerse yourself in the local culture, make connections with the community, and share your experiences to enrich your journey in this captivating and diverse country.

3. Health Insurance and Social Security

Securing appropriate health insurance and understanding the French social security system are paramount for expatriates moving to France. France offers a robust healthcare system that provides quality medical services to its residents and citizens. As an expatriate, it is essential to explore health insurance options and comply with social security requirements to ensure access to healthcare and financial protection.

The French healthcare system is renowned for its universal coverage and high standard of care. Residents and expatriates alike have access to an extensive network of hospitals, clinics, and healthcare professionals. Expatriates can choose between private health insurance and the French national health insurance system, known as Caisse Primaire d'Assurance Maladie (CPAM). Joining CPAM is a common choice for expatriates as it provides comprehensive coverage and cost-sharing for medical expenses.

To register with CPAM, you will need to submit certain documents, such as your residence permit, proof of address, and a valid bank account. Once registered, you will receive a Carte Vitale, a health insurance card that simplifies the reimbursement process for medical expenses. The Carte Vitale is essential for accessing medical services and ensuring seamless billing procedures.

In addition to the national health insurance, it is advisable to consider private health insurance to supplement your coverage. Private insurance can offer additional benefits, such as higher coverage limits, access to private hospitals, and coverage for specific medical services not fully covered by the public system.

Understanding the French social security system is crucial for compliance and financial planning. Social security contributions are mandatory for employees and self-employed individuals. These contributions fund various social benefits, such as healthcare, retirement pensions, family allowances, and unemployment benefits. Expatriates employed in France are typically subject to social security contributions, and their employers contribute on their behalf.

For individuals who are self-employed or freelancing, it is essential to determine their social security status and obligations. Some may be eligible for the auto-entrepreneur regime, a simplified system with reduced social security contributions for small businesses.

Expatriates from EU/EEA countries may have their social security contributions coordinated between France and their home country through the European Health Insurance Card (EHIC) or other agreements.

Complying with health insurance and social security requirements not only ensures access to quality healthcare but also provides financial security during unforeseen circumstances. Regularly review your insurance coverage and social security contributions to adapt to any changes in your employment status or personal circumstances.

In conclusion, Section 3 of this guide emphasizes the importance of health insurance and social security for expatriates in France. Understanding the French healthcare system and registering with CPAM or acquiring private health insurance is vital to access quality medical services. Complying with social security contributions is essential for financial protection and access to various social benefits. By proactively managing your health insurance and social security requirements, you can enjoy your life in France with peace of mind and the assurance of comprehensive healthcare coverage and financial support.

4. Taxation and Financial Obligations

Understanding the French tax system and fulfilling your financial obligations as an expatriate are essential aspects of successfully settling in France. France has a comprehensive tax system that includes income tax, property tax, and wealth tax. Navigating these tax regulations ensures compliance and financial stability during your time in the country.

Determining your tax residency status is the first step in understanding your tax obligations. As an expatriate, your tax residency status is typically determined by the duration and nature of your stay in France. If you spend more than 183 days in a calendar year in France or if your primary residence, professional activities, or economic interests are located in France, you may be considered a tax resident and subject to French income tax on your worldwide income.

Expatriates who qualify as tax residents in France are required to declare their income and assets annually. The French income tax system is progressive, meaning that higher income levels are subject to higher tax rates. Deductions and tax credits may apply to specific expenses, such as housing costs or dependent children.

If you have income from your home country, you may be subject to double taxation. France has tax treaties with many countries to prevent double taxation, allowing you to benefit from tax credits or exemptions. It is advisable to consult with a tax advisor or tax professional experienced in international taxation to ensure compliance and optimize your tax situation.

In addition to income tax, property tax is applicable to property owners in France. If you own property in France, you will be subject to the annual taxe foncière and, in some cases, the taxe d'habitation. Renters may also be subject to the taxe d'habitation.

Wealth tax, known as Impôt sur la Fortune Immobilière (IFI), is applicable to individuals with significant real estate assets in France. IFI applies to the net value of your real estate assets exceeding a certain threshold. Careful financial planning is necessary to assess whether you may be subject to IFI and to ensure compliance.

To facilitate tax filing and reporting, it is essential to keep detailed records of your income, expenses, and assets. Familiarize yourself with the tax filing deadlines and gather all necessary documentation to ensure accurate and timely submissions.

In conclusion, Section 4 of this guide highlights the significance of taxation and financial obligations for expatriates in France. Understanding the French tax system, determining tax residency status, and complying with income tax, property tax, and wealth tax requirements are essential for financial stability and compliance. Seeking professional tax advice and keeping accurate records will help optimize your tax situation and ensure a smooth financial experience during your stay in France. By proactively managing your tax and financial obligations, you can focus on enjoying your life in France and making the most of the diverse opportunities this captivating country has to offer.

5. Driving and Transportation

Navigating the transportation system in France is crucial for expatriates seeking mobility and independence. Whether you plan to drive or use public transportation, understanding the rules and options available will help you navigate the roads and cities effectively.

If you hold a valid driving license from an EU/EEA country, you can use it in France without any additional requirements. However, if you come from a non-EU/EEA country, you may need an International Driving Permit (IDP) to drive in France. The IDP is a translation of your home country's driving license and is generally valid for one year. Check the specific requirements based on your home country to ensure compliance.

Driving in France offers an excellent way to explore the countryside and remote areas. French roads are well-maintained, and the highway network, known as the Autoroute, allows for efficient travel between cities and regions. However, it is essential to familiarize yourself with French traffic rules and regulations to ensure safe driving. Speed limits, road signs, and driving etiquette may differ from what you are accustomed to in your home country.

In cities and urban areas, public transportation is a popular and convenient option for getting around. France has an extensive network of trains, trams, buses, and metros, making it easy to travel within cities and between regions. The national railway company, SNCF, operates high-speed trains (TGV) that connect major cities, providing a fast and efficient means of transportation.

To use public transportation, you can purchase individual tickets or opt for various transportation passes, such as Navigo in Paris or Carte Pastel in Toulouse, which offer unlimited travel within specific zones and timeframes. Public transportation is not only cost-effective but also eco-friendly, making it an attractive choice for many expatriates.

If you plan to reside in a city or urban area, consider the option of using bicycles or electric scooters for short-distance commutes. Many cities in France have implemented bike-sharing programs, allowing you to easily rent bicycles for short trips around town.

In addition to public transportation, ride-sharing services, such as Uber, are available in major cities, providing an alternative to taxis and public transportation.

As you explore transportation options in France, be aware of environmental regulations, especially in major cities. Some cities have implemented low-emission zones where specific vehicles may be restricted or subject to additional fees.

In conclusion, Section 5 of this guide highlights the importance of understanding driving and transportation options in France. If you plan to drive, ensure you have the necessary documents, such as an International Driving Permit if required. Familiarize yourself with French traffic rules and regulations for safe driving. Public transportation is a convenient and eco-friendly option, with an extensive network connecting cities and regions. Consider using bicycles, electric scooters, or ride-sharing services for short-distance commutes. By being well-informed about transportation choices, you can efficiently navigate France and enjoy the freedom of exploring this diverse and captivating country.

Chapter 3: Finding Accommodation

Finding suitable accommodation is a critical aspect of relocating to a new country. In Chapter 3, we will guide you through the process of finding accommodation in France, offering insights into different housing options, factors to consider when choosing a location, and tips for a successful house hunt. Whether you prefer city living, countryside charm, or coastal bliss, this chapter will help you find a place to call home in the enchanting country of France.

Section 1: Types of Accommodation in France

- Explore Different Housing Options: Learn about the variety of accommodation types available in France, including apartments, houses, studios, and lofts. Understand the unique characteristics of each option and consider which one best suits your lifestyle and needs.

- Temporary Accommodation: Discover short-term housing solutions, such as hotels, hostels, and furnished apartments, to use while you search for permanent accommodation. Learn how to book temporary stays and the best resources to find suitable options.

Section 2: Factors to Consider When Choosing a Location

- Prioritize Your Needs: Determine your lifestyle preferences and prioritize factors such as proximity to work or school, public transportation availability, access to amenities, safety, and neighborhood ambiance.

- City Living vs. Rural Charm: Understand the advantages and disadvantages of living in a city versus a rural area. Consider whether you prefer the vibrant atmosphere of urban centers or the tranquility of the countryside.

Section 3: House Hunting in France

- Online Resources: Explore popular online platforms and real estate websites to search for available properties in your desired location. Learn how to filter searches based on your budget and preferences.

- Working with Real Estate Agents: Understand the role of real estate agents in France and how they can assist you in finding the right accommodation. Learn how to contact and engage with real estate professionals to optimize your house hunting experience.

Section 4: Renting a Property

- Rental Market Overview: Gain insights into the rental market in France, including typical lease durations, security deposit requirements, and tenant rights and responsibilities.

- Documentation and Requirements: Prepare the necessary documents, such as proof of income, references, and identification, to streamline the rental application process.

- Negotiating the Lease: Learn about negotiating rental terms, including rent prices, maintenance responsibilities, and the possibility of furnished or unfurnished rentals.

Section 5: Buying a Property

- Understanding the Buying Process: Familiarize yourself with the steps involved in buying a property in France, from making an offer to completing the purchase at the notary's office.

- Financing and Mortgages: Explore financing options and mortgage possibilities for expatriates buying property in France. Understand the associated costs, taxes, and fees involved in property acquisition.

Section 6: Considerations for Expats

- Expatriate-Friendly Areas: Discover regions and cities known for their expatriate communities and amenities catering to international residents.

- Legal Considerations: Be aware of specific legal and tax implications for expatriates buying property in France. Seek professional advice to ensure compliance and avoid potential pitfalls.

By following the guidance provided in Chapter 3, you can navigate the process of finding accommodation in France with confidence. Whether you are renting or buying, understanding the housing options, considering essential factors, and being informed about legal and financial considerations will help you secure the perfect place to create your new home in this captivating and diverse country.

1. Types of Accommodation in France

France offers a wide range of accommodation options, catering to various lifestyles and preferences. Understanding the different types of housing available will help you choose the one that best suits your needs and enhances your experience of living in this beautiful country.

Apartments are a prevalent form of accommodation in urban areas and cities. They come in various sizes, from studios ideal for individuals or young couples to larger apartments suitable for families. Apartments can be found in traditional buildings with charming architectural features or modern high-rise complexes with contemporary amenities. Many apartments in cities offer the advantage of being centrally located, providing easy access to public transportation, shops, and cultural attractions.

Houses are an attractive option for those seeking more space, privacy, and a sense of community. In suburban and rural areas, houses often come with gardens or outdoor spaces, making them ideal for families or individuals who enjoy outdoor living. Traditional French houses, such as cottages or townhouses, exude charm and character, while newer properties may offer modern conveniences and energy-efficient features.

Studios are compact apartments typically consisting of one main living area, a small kitchenette, and a separate bathroom. Studios are an excellent choice for single individuals or young professionals who value simplicity and affordability. They are often located in central city areas, providing easy access to amenities and city life.

Lofts are spacious, open-plan living spaces usually converted from industrial buildings or warehouses. Lofts are prized for their modern and stylish design, featuring high ceilings, large windows, and exposed brick or steel beams. They appeal to individuals with a preference for contemporary living and creative spaces.

Furnished apartments cater to individuals looking for convenience and flexibility. These apartments come fully equipped with furniture and essential appliances, making them ideal for short-term stays or expatriates who don't want the hassle of furnishing a place from scratch. Furnished rentals are available in cities and tourist areas, and they often include utilities in the rent.

Temporary accommodation options include hotels, hostels, and serviced apartments. Hotels and hostels are suitable for short stays or during the initial period of house hunting. Serviced apartments offer more space and amenities, such as housekeeping and concierge services, providing a comfortable and hotel-like experience for extended stays.

In conclusion, Section 1 of this guide provides valuable insights into the different types of accommodation available in France. Apartments, houses, studios, and lofts cater to a diverse range of preferences, whether you prefer the urban buzz of the city or the tranquility of the countryside. Temporary accommodation options are available for short-term stays while searching for permanent housing. By understanding the various types of accommodation, you can make an informed decision that aligns with your lifestyle and enhances your experience of living in this enchanting and culturally rich country.

2. Factors to Consider When Choosing a Location

Choosing the right location for your accommodation in France is a crucial decision that can significantly impact your daily life and overall experience in the country. Consideration of various factors will help you identify a location that aligns with your lifestyle, priorities, and preferences.

Proximity to work or school is a top consideration when choosing a location. Living close to your workplace or educational institution can reduce commute times and expenses, giving you more time to enjoy leisure activities and explore your surroundings. Access to reliable public transportation is also essential, especially if you do not plan to drive regularly.

The availability of amenities and services is another vital factor. Consider the proximity to grocery stores, pharmacies, hospitals, gyms, parks, and cultural venues. Living in an area with easy access to daily necessities and recreational facilities can enhance your quality of life.

Safety is a paramount concern for anyone looking for a new home. Research the safety record and reputation of the neighborhoods you are considering. Opt for areas with a low crime rate and a reputation for being secure, especially if you plan to live with family or value peace of mind.

The ambiance and character of the neighborhood play a significant role in the overall living experience. Some individuals may prefer the vibrant atmosphere of city centers with bustling markets, cafes, and cultural events. Others might seek the tranquility and charm of residential neighborhoods in the suburbs or countryside.

Consider the availability of schools and educational institutions if you have children or plan to pursue further education. Living near quality schools can be advantageous for families, while proximity to universities and language schools may be crucial for students.

Affordability is a significant factor that impacts your choice of location. Housing costs can vary widely across different regions and neighborhoods in France. Balancing your budget with your desired location is essential for financial stability and overall satisfaction with your accommodation.

City living and rural charm offer distinct experiences, and both have their merits. Urban centers provide a wealth of cultural activities, dining options, and career opportunities. On the other hand, rural areas offer a slower pace of life, natural beauty, and a sense of community. Consider which environment aligns better with your lifestyle and personal preferences.

Engaging with the local community can significantly impact your sense of belonging. Explore neighborhoods with active social scenes and community events to facilitate interaction with locals and fellow expatriates. Being part of a welcoming and inclusive community can make your experience in France even more enriching.

In conclusion, Section 2 of this guide highlights essential factors to consider when choosing a location for your accommodation in France. Proximity to work or school, access to amenities, safety, neighborhood ambiance, educational opportunities, affordability, and the type of environment are all important considerations. By carefully evaluating these factors and aligning them with your priorities and lifestyle, you can identify the ideal location that will make your time in France a rewarding and fulfilling experience.

3. House Hunting in France

House hunting in France can be an exciting yet challenging process, especially for expatriates unfamiliar with the local real estate market. Section 3 of this guide provides valuable insights and tips to streamline your house-hunting experience and help you find your dream home in this beautiful country.

Online resources are a valuable starting point for your house hunt. Numerous real estate websites and online platforms offer a wide selection of properties available for sale or rent in various regions of France. These websites allow you to filter your searches based on your budget, preferred location, property type, and other specific criteria, making it easier to identify potential options that match your requirements. Utilizing these online resources gives you a comprehensive overview of the current housing market and helps you identify trends and patterns in different areas.

Working with a real estate agent can be highly beneficial, especially if you are new to the country or not familiar with the local language and regulations. Real estate agents in France are experienced professionals who can guide you through the house-hunting process, offer valuable advice on neighborhoods and property options, and negotiate on your behalf. Ensure that you choose a reputable and licensed agent who has experience working with expatriates and understands your unique needs and preferences.

As you explore potential properties, consider conducting thorough site visits to assess each property's suitability. Pay attention to essential features such as the condition of the property, the surrounding neighborhood, accessibility to amenities and transportation, and the overall ambiance. Take note of any potential renovation or maintenance requirements to factor these costs into your decision-making process.

For rental properties, be prepared with the necessary documentation when submitting a rental application. Landlords typically require proof of income, references, identification, and sometimes a security deposit. Demonstrating your reliability and financial stability can increase your chances of securing your desired rental property.

Negotiation is an essential part of the house-hunting process, particularly for buying a property. Be prepared to negotiate the price and terms of the sale, especially if you are working with a real estate agent who can represent your interests during the negotiation process. Remember that property prices in France are often negotiable, and a successful negotiation can lead to a more favorable deal.

In conclusion, Section 3 offers valuable guidance on house hunting in France. Utilize online resources and work with experienced real estate agents to maximize your options and make informed decisions. Thoroughly assess properties during site visits and factor in renovation or maintenance costs when considering your budget. Be prepared with the necessary documentation for rental applications and be open to negotiation when buying a property. With these insights and proactive approaches, you can embark on a successful house-hunting journey and find the perfect accommodation that will make your experience in France truly unforgettable.

4. Renting a Property

Renting a property in France is a common and flexible option for many expatriates, providing a convenient and relatively straightforward way to secure accommodation. In Section 4 of this guide, we will explore the rental process in France, including an overview of the rental market, essential documentation and requirements, and tips for negotiating the lease terms.

Understanding the rental market in France is essential for a successful house-hunting experience. Rental prices can vary significantly based on the location, property type, and market demand. Researching rental trends in your desired area will give you a realistic expectation of rental costs and help you identify opportunities that align with your budget.

When beginning your rental search, be prepared with the necessary documentation to facilitate the application process. Landlords typically request proof of income, such as pay stubs or employment contracts, to ensure you can afford the rental property. Providing references from previous landlords or employers can strengthen your application and demonstrate your reliability as a tenant. Additionally, having a valid form of identification, such as a passport or residence permit, is essential for rental applications.

Rental contracts in France usually come in two main formats: the unfurnished rental contract (bail d'habitation vide) and the furnished rental contract (bail d'habitation meublée). Unfurnished contracts generally have longer durations, typically lasting for three years, while furnished contracts tend to be shorter, usually lasting for one year. It is essential to carefully read and understand the terms and conditions of the rental contract before signing, as it will outline your rights and responsibilities as a tenant.

The security deposit is a standard requirement in rental agreements in France. It serves as a guarantee for the landlord in case of any damages or unpaid rent during your tenancy. The maximum amount of the security deposit is typically limited to one or two months' rent. It is important to keep records of the property's condition and any pre-existing damages when you move in to avoid any disputes when it is time to refund the deposit.

Negotiating the lease terms is a common practice in the rental market, especially for long-term rentals. If you are renting directly from the property owner, there may be some flexibility in negotiating the monthly rent or specific terms of the lease. However, if you are renting through a real estate agency, the negotiation room might be more limited. It is always worth discussing your preferences and needs with the landlord or agency to see if there are any potential adjustments that can be made to the lease.

In conclusion, Section 4 provides comprehensive insights into renting a property in France. Familiarizing yourself with the rental market, preparing the necessary documentation, and carefully reviewing the rental contract are vital steps to ensure a smooth and successful rental experience. Negotiating lease terms and understanding the security deposit process are additional aspects to consider when securing your ideal rental property. By being well-prepared and informed, you can confidently navigate the rental process and find the perfect place to call home during your time in France.

5. Buying a Property

Purchasing a property in France can be a rewarding and long-term investment, offering a sense of permanence and stability. In Section 5 of this guide, we delve into the process of buying a property in France, including an overview of the buying process, financing options, associated costs, and legal considerations.

The buying process in France typically begins with property search and selection. Utilize online resources, real estate agencies, and property listings to explore available options. Engage the services of a licensed and reputable real estate agent who can guide you through the search and provide valuable insights into the local property market.

Before proceeding with a property purchase, it is essential to determine your budget and explore financing options. If you require a mortgage to purchase a property, research different lenders and mortgage options to find the best terms and interest rates. Getting pre-approved for a mortgage can give you a competitive edge when making offers on properties.

Once you find a property that meets your criteria, the next step is to make an offer. In France, property prices are negotiable, and sellers often expect potential buyers to negotiate the final price. The negotiation process involves reaching an agreement on the sale price, as well as any other terms and conditions, such as the inclusion of furniture or appliances.

When the seller accepts your offer, you will move on to the formalities of the sale. Both parties sign a preliminary sales agreement called the "compromis de vente," which outlines the terms of the sale. At this stage, you will typically pay a deposit, usually around 5-10% of the property's purchase price. The "compromis de vente" is a legally binding document, and backing out of the sale after signing may result in financial penalties.

Before completing the sale, a notary, appointed by the buyer, conducts various legal and administrative tasks to ensure the property's legality and clear title. The notary prepares the final contract, known as the "acte de vente," which is signed by both parties in the presence of the notary. On the completion date, the remaining purchase price and associated fees are paid, and the property officially changes ownership.

It is crucial to be aware of the costs associated with buying a property in France. In addition to the purchase price, buyers must budget for various expenses, such as notary fees, registration fees, and property transfer tax (also known as "droits de mutation"). These costs can add several percentage points to the total purchase price, so factoring them into your budget is essential.

Understanding the legal and tax implications of property ownership in France is vital for a smooth and compliant purchase. Seek advice from a qualified legal professional or notary to ensure you are aware of all the obligations, rights, and responsibilities associated with property ownership.

In conclusion, Section 5 provides comprehensive guidance on buying a property in France. From property search and selection to negotiation, financing, and the final sale, understanding the buying process is essential for a successful property purchase. Being well-informed about associated costs, legal considerations, and tax implications will help you make a sound investment decision and achieve your dream of owning a property in this captivating country.

6. Considerations for Expats

Moving to a new country as an expatriate comes with its unique set of considerations and challenges. In Section 6 of this guide, we address specific aspects that expatriates should be mindful of when relocating to France, ensuring a smooth transition and a fulfilling experience in their new home.

Expatriate-Friendly Areas: Some regions and cities in France are particularly popular among expatriates due to their diverse communities, international schools, and amenities catering to foreigners. Paris, Lyon, Nice, and Toulouse are among the cities with vibrant expatriate communities. Researching and considering these expatriate-friendly areas can facilitate your integration into the local culture and help you establish connections with like-minded individuals.

Legal Considerations: As an expatriate, it is essential to be aware of specific legal considerations regarding your residency status and the necessary paperwork for living in France. Ensure that you have a valid visa or residence permit that allows you to reside in the country for your intended duration. Staying informed about immigration regulations and renewing your documentation when necessary will help you avoid legal complications.

Language Barrier: While English is commonly spoken in urban areas and tourist destinations, French remains the official language of the country. Learning the basics of the French language can significantly enhance your daily interactions, facilitate integration, and demonstrate your respect for the local culture. Consider enrolling in language courses or using language apps to improve your language skills.

Healthcare and Insurance: Understanding the French healthcare system and securing appropriate health insurance are vital aspects of expat life. Expatriates from EU/EEA countries can access healthcare through the European Health Insurance Card (EHIC) or private health insurance. Non-EU/EEA expatriates may need to register with the French national health insurance system or opt for private health insurance. Researching the available options and their coverage is essential for ensuring access to quality healthcare during your stay in France.

Cultural Adaptation: Embracing the French way of life and cultural norms can lead to a more enriching experience as an expatriate. Familiarize yourself with French customs, etiquette, and social norms. Embrace local traditions, festivals, and cuisine to immerse yourself in the rich cultural heritage of France. Engaging with the local community and participating in cultural events can also foster meaningful connections and friendships.

Banking and Financial Considerations: Opening a bank account in France is a practical step for managing your finances and daily transactions. Research different banks and their services to find one that suits your needs. Familiarize yourself with French banking procedures, such as direct debits and online banking, to ease your financial management.

Networking and Expatriate Communities: Connecting with other expatriates can provide valuable support and guidance during your transition to France. Expatriate communities often organize social events, networking opportunities, and support groups. Engaging with these communities can help you feel more at home and provide insights into the expatriate experience in France.

In conclusion, Section 6 addresses key considerations for expatriates moving to France. By being aware of expatriate-friendly areas, legal requirements, the language barrier, healthcare and insurance options, cultural adaptation, banking procedures, and the support of expatriate communities, you can navigate your new life in France with confidence and make the most of your expatriate journey. Embrace the opportunity to immerse yourself in the French culture, build meaningful connections, and enjoy the unique experiences that this diverse and captivating country has to offer.

Chapter 4: Education and Healthcare

Chapter 4 of this guide delves into two vital aspects of expatriate life in France: education and healthcare. Moving to a new country with a family or as a student requires a comprehensive understanding of the education system and available healthcare services. This chapter aims to provide insights into the French education system, options for international students, navigating the healthcare system, and obtaining appropriate health insurance coverage.

Section 1: Education in France

- Overview of the French Education System: Understand the structure of the education system in France, from primary to secondary education, and the different levels of higher education.

- International Schools: Explore the options for international schools in France, offering curriculums in multiple languages and catering to the needs of expatriate children.

- Public vs. Private Education: Compare public and private schools in France, considering factors such as cost, curriculum, and language of instruction.

- Enrolling Your Child in School: Learn about the enrollment process for expatriate children in both public and private schools, including necessary documents and considerations.

Section 2: Education for International Students

- Higher Education in France: Discover the opportunities for international students to pursue higher education in France, including undergraduate and graduate programs at universities and specialized institutions.

- Admission Process and Requirements: Understand the application process for international students, including admission requirements, language proficiency tests, and visa procedures.

- Scholarships and Financial Aid: Explore scholarship opportunities and financial aid options available to international students studying in France.

Section 3: Healthcare in France

- Overview of the French Healthcare System: Gain insights into the French healthcare system, which is known for its universal coverage and high-quality medical services.

- Accessing Healthcare Services: Understand how to access healthcare services as an expatriate, including registering with the French national health insurance system and finding doctors or specialists.

- Emergency Medical Services: Familiarize yourself with emergency medical services and the process for seeking medical assistance during urgent situations.

Section 4: Health Insurance for Expatriates

- Health Insurance Options: Explore health insurance options for expatriates in France, including the French national health insurance system (CPAM), private health insurance, and international health insurance plans.

- Obtaining Health Insurance Coverage: Learn how to obtain health insurance coverage, what documents are required, and the process for submitting claims.

By delving into Chapter 4, expatriates in France can gain a comprehensive understanding of the education system and healthcare services in the country. Whether you are moving with a family or studying as an international student, this chapter will equip you with the knowledge to make informed decisions about education and healthcare, ensuring a smooth and fulfilling experience during your time in France.

1. Education in France

The French education system is renowned for its rigorous curriculum and emphasis on academic excellence. In Section 1 of this guide, we provide a comprehensive overview of the education system in France, from primary to higher education, and the options available to expatriate families seeking education for their children.

The French education system is divided into several stages. At the preschool level, children aged three to six attend école maternelle, where they focus on developing social and cognitive skills through play and early learning activities.

Primary education, known as école élémentaire, starts at age six and lasts for five years. During this stage, students study a range of subjects, including mathematics, French language, history, geography, and physical education.

At the end of primary education, students take an examination called the Certificat d'Études Primaires (CEP) to assess their academic progress. Successful completion of the CEP allows students to progress to collège, the next stage of education.

Collège covers four years of study, from ages 11 to 15. Here, students follow a more structured curriculum, including additional subjects such as foreign languages, science, and technology. At the end of collège, students take the Diplôme National du Brevet (DNB) examination.

After collège, students have the option to pursue either general or vocational education. Those opting for general education continue to lycée, where they undertake the baccalauréat (commonly known as the bac) examination after three years. The bac is a critical examination that determines university eligibility.

France also offers private and international schools that cater to expatriate families. International schools provide curriculums in multiple languages, including English, and often follow internationally recognized education systems such as the International Baccalaureate (IB) or the British or American curriculum. These schools are popular choices for expatriate children, as they provide continuity in education and accommodate language differences.

The choice between public and private education in France is an important consideration for expatriate families. Public schools generally follow the French national curriculum and offer education in French. Private schools may provide alternative educational approaches and may offer instruction in other languages. Private schools often have tuition fees, whereas public schools are tuition-free.

Enrolling expatriate children in French schools typically requires specific documents, such as proof of residency, identification, and medical records. Some schools may require additional language assessments to determine language proficiency. Researching and understanding the enrollment process is crucial for expatriate families to ensure a smooth transition for their children into the French education system.

In conclusion, Section 1 provides a comprehensive overview of education in France, from preschool to higher education. The French education system is well-structured, emphasizing academic development and offering multiple opportunities for students to progress in their studies. Expatriate families have the option to choose between public and private schools, and international schools cater to those seeking continuity in education. Understanding the enrollment process and educational options will help expatriate families make informed decisions about their children's education, ensuring a successful and rewarding experience in the French education system.

2. Education for International Students

France has long been a favored destination for international students seeking high-quality education and cultural enrichment. In Section 2 of this guide, we delve into the opportunities and considerations for international students pursuing higher education in France.

France boasts a prestigious higher education system, offering a wide range of programs in various fields of study. International students have the opportunity to pursue undergraduate, graduate, and doctoral degrees at renowned universities and specialized institutions across the country. Many French universities are ranked among the top institutions globally, making them attractive choices for international students seeking academic excellence.

The admission process for international students in France typically involves submitting an application directly to the university or through the online platform, Campus France. Each institution may have specific admission requirements, which often include academic transcripts, language proficiency tests (such as the Test de Connaissance du Français - TCF), letters of recommendation, and a statement of purpose. It is essential to check the specific requirements of each program and institution to ensure a complete and successful application.

For programs taught in French, international students must demonstrate a sufficient level of French language proficiency to fully engage in their studies. Some universities may require students to take a French language course or pass a language test before starting their academic program. However, many universities in France offer programs taught in English, particularly at the graduate level, to accommodate the growing number of international students seeking English-taught courses.

Financial considerations are crucial for international students planning to study in France. Tuition fees for international students vary depending on the institution and the level of study. Public universities in France typically offer lower tuition fees compared to private institutions. Additionally, scholarships and financial aid opportunities are available for international students through various French government programs, university scholarships, and international organizations.

Living expenses, including accommodation, food, transportation, and other personal costs, should also be factored into a student's budget. Many universities have student services that can provide guidance on finding affordable housing options and accessing financial aid resources.

France is a country known for its rich cultural heritage and vibrant lifestyle. International students have the opportunity to experience a unique blend of academic excellence and cultural immersion. Engaging in extracurricular activities, joining student organizations, and exploring local events and traditions can enhance the student experience and facilitate cross-cultural interactions.

In conclusion, Section 2 offers valuable insights into education opportunities for international students in France. The country's higher education system is esteemed globally, with diverse programs and institutions catering to a wide range of academic interests. Understanding the admission process, language requirements, and financial considerations will help international students navigate their path to studying in France. Embracing the cultural richness and embracing new experiences will make studying in France a transformative and unforgettable chapter in an international student's academic journey.

3. Healthcare in France

The French healthcare system is highly regarded for its comprehensive coverage and quality of medical services. In Section 3 of this guide, we provide a comprehensive overview of healthcare in France, including the structure of the healthcare system, accessing healthcare services, and emergency medical care.

The French healthcare system is based on the principle of universal coverage, ensuring that all residents, including expatriates, have access to essential medical services. It is primarily funded through a combination of social security contributions, government funding, and patient copayments. The system is overseen by the French Ministry of Social Affairs and Health.

To access healthcare services in France, expatriates should register with the French national health insurance system, known as Caisse Primaire d'Assurance Maladie (CPAM). Registration typically requires providing proof of residency, identification, and other relevant documents. Once registered, individuals receive a Carte Vitale, a health in-surance card that simplifies the reimbursement process for medical ex-penses.

French residents have the freedom to choose their healthcare providers, including general practitioners, specialists, and hospitals. Visits to doctors and medical specialists are generally reimbursed by the national health insurance, with patients paying a portion of the cost as a copayment. The reimbursement rates and copayments may vary de-pending on the type of medical service and whether the provider is part of the public or private healthcare sector.

In addition to general medical services, France also offers a range of specialized medical facilities, including renowned research hospitals and treatment centers. Access to quality medical care is readily available throughout the country, with well-developed healthcare infrastructure in both urban and rural areas.

In emergency situations, the French healthcare system provides swift and efficient medical assistance. The national emergency tele-phone number in France is 112, which connects callers to emergency medical services (SAMU). In urgent cases, ambulances and medical teams are dispatched promptly to provide necessary medical care.

While the French healthcare system offers extensive coverage, some individuals may choose to supplement their coverage with private health insurance. Private health insurance plans can provide additional benefits, such as coverage for services not fully reimbursed by the na-tional health insurance, faster access to specialists, and more compre-hensive dental and vision care.

Expatriates should carefully consider their healthcare needs and preferences when choosing health insurance coverage. International health insurance plans tailored for expatriates are available and can pro-vide coverage both in France and for international travel.

In conclusion, Section 3 provides a comprehensive overview of healthcare in France. The French healthcare system is renowned for its universal coverage and high-quality medical services. By registering with the national health insurance system, expatriates can access a wide range of healthcare services throughout the country. Additionally, private health insurance options are available to supplement coverage and cater to individual healthcare needs. The efficient emergency medical services ensure that individuals receive timely medical attention in urgent situations. Overall, the healthcare system in France provides peace of mind and ensures that residents, including expatriates, have access to quality medical care during their stay in the country.

4. Health Insurance for Expatriates

Health insurance is a vital consideration for expatriates living in France, providing financial security and access to comprehensive healthcare services. In Section 4 of this guide, we explore the various health insurance options available to expatriates, ensuring they can make informed decisions about their healthcare coverage.

Expatriates in France have multiple health insurance options to consider, each with its own advantages and coverage levels. The primary option is the French national health insurance system, known as Caisse Primaire d'Assurance Maladie (CPAM). Expatriates who are working or residing in France for an extended period may be eligible to register with CPAM and benefit from the country's universal healthcare coverage. CPAM provides reimbursement for a wide range of medical services and treatments, ensuring that expatriates have access to quality healthcare without bearing the full financial burden.

However, some expatriates may opt for private health insurance to complement the coverage provided by CPAM. Private health insurance plans offer additional benefits, such as coverage for medical services not fully reimbursed by CPAM, access to a broader network of healthcare providers, and shorter waiting times for specialist appointments. International health insurance plans designed for expatriates can be especially beneficial, as they provide coverage not only in France but also during travels to other countries.

Private health insurance plans for expatriates can be tailored to suit individual healthcare needs and preferences. Expatriates can choose from various coverage levels, including basic plans for essential medical services or comprehensive plans that include additional benefits like dental, vision care, and alternative treatments. Tailoring health insurance coverage allows expatriates to select a plan that aligns with their specific healthcare requirements and budget.

Expatriates should carefully review the terms and conditions of their health insurance policies, including coverage limits, exclusions, and the process for submitting claims. Understanding the policy's coverage and reimbursement procedures will ensure that expatriates can effectively utilize their health insurance when seeking medical care.

Before choosing health insurance coverage, expatriates should also consider factors such as their length of stay in France, pre-existing medical conditions, and the healthcare needs of their family members. Seeking advice from an insurance broker or consultant specializing in expatriate health insurance can be helpful in navigating the various options and selecting the most suitable plan.

In conclusion, Section 4 highlights the importance of health insurance for expatriates living in France. While the French national health insurance system provides comprehensive coverage, private health insurance can offer additional benefits and tailor-made solutions for individual healthcare needs. Expatriates have the flexibility to choose from various health insurance options, including international health insurance plans that provide coverage both in France and internationally. By carefully assessing their healthcare requirements and exploring the available insurance options, expatriates can ensure they have the appropriate health insurance coverage to safeguard their well-being during their stay in France.

Chapter 5: Employment and Entrepreneurship

Chapter 5 of this guide explores the opportunities and considerations for expatriates in France regarding employment and entrepreneurship. Whether seeking job opportunities or starting a business venture, this chapter provides insights into the French job market, work permits, self-employment options, and the process of establishing a business in the country.

Section 1: Employment in France

- Job Market Overview: Gain an understanding of the French job market, including key industries, in-demand professions, and the current employment landscape.

- Work Permits and Visas: Learn about the different types of work permits and visas available to expatriates, the application process, and the requirements for working legally in France.

- Job Search Strategies: Explore effective job search strategies, including networking, online job portals, recruitment agencies, and attending job fairs.

Section 2: Self-Employment and Freelancing

- Self-Employment Options: Consider the possibilities for self-employment and freelancing in France, from setting up as an independent contractor to registering as an auto-entrepreneur (micro-entrepreneur).

- Tax and Legal Considerations: Understand the tax implications and legal requirements of being self-employed or a freelancer, including registering a business, obtaining the necessary permits, and managing tax obligations.

Section 3: Starting a Business in France

- Business Types and Legal Structures: Explore the various business types and legal structures available for entrepreneurs in France, such as SARL (Société à Responsabilité Limitée) and SAS (Société par Actions Simplifiée).

- Business Plan and Funding: Learn about the importance of creating a solid business plan and exploring funding options for starting a business, including bank loans, government grants, and venture capital.

- Registration and Administrative Procedures: Navigate the process of registering a business in France, including obtaining a SIRET number, business licenses, and adhering to French labor laws.

Section 4: Working Conditions and Benefits

- Labor Laws and Employee Rights: Familiarize yourself with French labor laws, including working hours, minimum wage, vacation entitlement, and employee benefits.

- Social Security and Healthcare: Understand the social security system in France, including contributions and entitlements to healthcare, retirement, and other social benefits.

Section 5: Networking and Professional Development

- Networking Opportunities: Discover avenues for networking with professionals and industry peers in France, such as attending industry events, joining professional organizations, and using online networking platforms.

- Professional Development: Embrace opportunities for professional growth and skills enhancement through workshops, seminars, and continuing education programs offered in France.

In conclusion, Chapter 5 provides comprehensive insights into employment and entrepreneurship in France for expatriates. From exploring the job market and work permits to understanding self-employment options and starting a business, expatriates have a range of opportunities to pursue their career goals in this dynamic country. Adhering to legal requirements, understanding working conditions and benefits, and engaging in networking and professional development activities will contribute to a successful and rewarding career or entrepreneurial journey in France.

1. Employment in France

France offers a diverse and dynamic job market with opportunities across various industries and professions. In Section 1 of this guide, we provide a comprehensive overview of employment in France, including the job market landscape, work permits and visas for expatriates, and effective job search strategies.

The French job market is characterized by a mix of traditional industries, such as manufacturing, tourism, and agriculture, as well as emerging sectors like technology, renewable energy, and finance. Major cities like Paris, Lyon, and Marseille serve as economic hubs, attracting both local and international companies, and providing a wide array of employment prospects.

Expatriates interested in working in France must secure the appropriate work permit or visa to legally work in the country. The process of obtaining a work permit may vary depending on factors such as the expatriate's country of origin, the nature of the employment, and the duration of the intended stay. Employers hiring expatriates from outside the European Union (EU) often play a crucial role in facilitating the work permit application process. Expatriates should familiarize themselves with the different types of work permits and visas available to ensure compliance with French immigration regulations.

Job search strategies in France can be enhanced through various channels. Networking is particularly valuable, as personal connections play a significant role in the French business culture. Attending industry events, professional conferences, and job fairs allows expatriates to build connections with potential employers and industry peers. Online job portals and recruitment agencies also serve as valuable resources for discovering job opportunities tailored to an expatriate's skills and qualifications.

France offers a diverse range of employment opportunities, from entry-level positions to executive roles. Fluency in French is often an advantage, especially for roles requiring extensive interactions with

French-speaking clients or colleagues. However, in multinational companies or English-speaking sectors, proficiency in English may suffice.

In addition to traditional employment, many expatriates explore the option of self-employment or freelancing in France. This path offers flexibility and the opportunity to manage one's own business or consultancy. The status of auto-entrepreneur (micro-entrepreneur) is particularly popular for those looking to establish a small business with simplified administrative requirements.

In conclusion, Section 1 provides a comprehensive overview of employment in France for expatriates. The French job market offers a wide range of opportunities in diverse industries and sectors. Securing the appropriate work permit or visa is crucial for legal employment in the country, and networking is a valuable strategy for building professional connections. The option of self-employment or freelancing is also available for those seeking entrepreneurship and flexibility in their careers. By understanding the nuances of the job market, work permits, and effective job search strategies, expatriates can confidently pursue their career aspirations and make the most of their professional journey in France.

2. Self-Employment and Freelancing

Self-employment and freelancing in France offer attractive opportunities for expatriates seeking independence and flexibility in their careers. In Section 2 of this guide, we explore the possibilities and considerations for expatriates who wish to work for themselves and navigate the intricacies of being self-employed or a freelancer in France.

Becoming self-employed in France involves setting up as an independent contractor or establishing a small business. Expatriates can choose to register as an auto-entrepreneur (micro-entrepreneur), a simplified status designed for small-scale business activities. The auto-entrepreneur status allows individuals to benefit from reduced administrative burdens, simplified tax procedures, and a flat-rate tax system based on their turnover. This option is particularly appealing to expatriates looking to launch a small business or provide freelance services while keeping their administrative tasks streamlined.

It is essential for expatriates to understand the tax and legal implications of being self-employed or a freelancer in France. As self-employed individuals, expatriates are responsible for their social security contributions, income tax, and other mandatory contributions. They should also keep accurate records of their business-related expenses and income for tax purposes. Seeking guidance from an accountant or tax advisor who specializes in the French tax system is highly advisable to ensure compliance and optimize tax obligations.

Freelancers and self-employed individuals in France can operate in various industries, including consulting, creative services, IT, and language instruction, among others. Fluency in French can be beneficial for certain freelance roles that require communication with French clients or local businesses. However, in some industries and remote work arrangements, proficiency in English may be sufficient.

Networking is an essential aspect of self-employment and freelancing in France. Building professional connections can lead to potential clients and collaborations. Engaging in networking events, industry meet-ups, and online communities can expand an expatriate's reach and open up new opportunities for their self-employed ventures.

Apart from the auto-entrepreneur status, expatriates who aspire to establish larger businesses or startups can explore other legal structures, such as SARL (Société à Responsabilité Limitée) or SAS (Société par Actions Simplifiée). Each legal structure has its advantages and requirements, which should be carefully considered when starting a business in France.

In conclusion, Section 2 provides valuable insights into self-employment and freelancing opportunities for expatriates in France. Registering as an auto-entrepreneur offers a simple and practical route for small-scale businesses and freelancers to establish themselves and benefit from the French social security system. Understanding the tax and legal obligations of self-employment is essential for managing one's business affairs effectively. Engaging in networking and choosing the appropriate legal structure for larger businesses contribute to a successful and fulfilling self-employed or freelance career in France. By embracing entrepreneurship and seizing the advantages of self-employment, expatriates can leverage their skills and talents to thrive in the French business landscape.

3. Starting a Business in France

France is a thriving hub for entrepreneurship, and Section 3 of this guide provides comprehensive insights into the process of starting a business in the country. From choosing a business type to navigating administrative procedures, expatriates considering entrepreneurship in France will find valuable guidance in this section.

One of the first steps in starting a business in France is choosing the most suitable legal structure. The most common options include SARL (Société à Responsabilité Limitée), SAS (Société par Actions Simplifiée), and the auto-entrepreneur (micro-entrepreneur) status. Each legal structure has its advantages and implications for liability, taxation, and administrative requirements. The choice of legal structure should align with the nature and scale of the business, the number of owners or shareholders, and long-term objectives.

The next critical aspect is creating a comprehensive business plan. A well-structured business plan outlines the company's mission, target market, marketing strategies, financial projections, and operational plans. A solid business plan is not only essential for attracting potential investors or securing financing but also serves as a roadmap for the business's growth and development.

Registering a business in France involves several administrative procedures. Expatriates must obtain a SIRET number, which is a unique identification number for businesses. Additionally, depending on the type of business, they may need to apply for specific licenses or permits to operate legally in certain industries.

Complying with French labor laws is crucial when starting a business that hires employees. Understanding regulations related to working hours, minimum wage, vacation entitlement, and employee benefits is essential for ensuring a fair and compliant work environment.

To finance their startup ventures, expatriates can explore various funding options. Bank loans, government grants, venture capital, and angel investors are some of the avenues available to secure financial support for the business. Networking with potential investors and attending entrepreneurship events can help entrepreneurs connect with funding opportunities.

Apart from legal and financial considerations, entrepreneurs should also consider the market potential and competition for their products or services. Conducting market research and understanding customer preferences and needs will contribute to the business's success and competitiveness.

Throughout the process of starting a business in France, seeking guidance from professionals, such as lawyers, accountants, or business advisors, is highly recommended. These experts can assist with legal paperwork, financial planning, and navigating the intricacies of the French business landscape.

In conclusion, Section 3 offers valuable guidance for expatriates seeking to embark on an entrepreneurial journey in France. From choosing the appropriate legal structure and creating a robust business plan to navigating administrative procedures and securing funding, starting a business requires careful planning and execution. Complying with labor laws and conducting market research are essential components of a successful business venture. By seeking professional advice and leveraging the vibrant entrepreneurial ecosystem in France, expatriates can turn their business ideas into thriving enterprises in this dynamic and innovative country.

4. Working Conditions and Benefits

In Section 4 of this guide, we delve into the working conditions and benefits that expatriates can expect while working in France. The French labor market is characterized by a strong emphasis on employee rights and welfare, providing a favorable work environment for both locals and expatriates.

French labor laws govern various aspects of employment, ensuring that employees are protected and treated fairly. The standard working week in France is 35 hours, although some industries or job positions may have different arrangements. Overtime work is regulated, and employees are entitled to additional pay or compensatory time off for extra hours worked beyond the standard weekly limit.

The minimum wage in France is set by law and is adjusted regularly to keep up with the cost of living. Employers are required to pay their employees at least the minimum wage, which provides a decent standard of living for workers in the country.

One of the essential benefits for employees in France is the generous vacation entitlement. Full-time employees are typically entitled to five weeks of paid vacation per year, offering ample opportunities for rest and relaxation. French law also provides for paid sick leave and maternity/paternity leave, ensuring that employees have support during times of illness or when starting a family.

Social security in France is a comprehensive system that covers various aspects of employee welfare. This system provides healthcare coverage, retirement benefits, unemployment benefits, family allowances, and other social benefits. Both employers and employees contribute to the social security system through payroll deductions, ensuring that individuals have access to essential services and financial support when needed.

In addition to legal benefits, many employers offer additional perks to attract and retain talent. These perks may include private health insurance, meal vouchers, transportation allowances, and opportunities for professional development and career advancement.

The French business culture emphasizes a healthy work-life balance, and companies often promote employee well-being through various initiatives. Flexible work arrangements, telecommuting options, and family-friendly policies are becoming more prevalent in many workplaces.

Expatriates should be aware of their rights and benefits as employees in France and understand their employment contracts thoroughly. Employers are generally required to provide written employment contracts outlining the terms of employment, including salary, working hours, benefits, and other relevant details.

In conclusion, Section 4 highlights the favorable working conditions and benefits that expatriates can enjoy while working in France. The French labor laws prioritize employee rights, including fair working hours, minimum wage, and generous vacation entitlement. The social security system provides comprehensive coverage, and employers often offer additional perks to enhance the overall work experience. Embracing the French emphasis on work-life balance, expatriates can look forward to a fulfilling and rewarding work environment while pursuing their career aspirations in this diverse and vibrant country.

5. Networking and Professional Development

In Section 5 of this guide, we explore the significance of networking and professional development for expatriates in France. Building a strong professional network and investing in continuous growth and learning are essential elements for career advancement and personal development in this dynamic country.

Networking plays a crucial role in the French business culture, where personal connections and relationships are highly valued. Expatriates can expand their professional network by actively engaging in various networking opportunities. Attending industry events, business conferences, and seminars provides avenues for meeting potential clients, collaborators, and mentors. Additionally, joining professional organizations and networking groups related to one's industry or interests can foster valuable connections within the local business community.

Online networking platforms and social media also offer valuable resources for expatriates to connect with professionals in their field. LinkedIn, in particular, is widely used in France for professional networking and job searches. Maintaining a well-curated LinkedIn profile and engaging in relevant discussions can raise an expatriate's visibility and open up new opportunities for career growth.

Professional development is equally critical for expatriates seeking to excel in their careers. France offers a diverse range of workshops, seminars, and training programs across various industries. These opportunities allow expatriates to enhance their skills, stay updated with industry trends, and demonstrate a commitment to continuous learning, which is highly valued by employers.

Language proficiency is an essential aspect of professional development for expatriates in France. While English is commonly spoken in multinational companies and certain industries, fluency in French is a significant advantage, especially for roles requiring regular interactions with local clients or colleagues. Expatriates can consider language courses or language exchange programs to improve their French skills and further integrate into the local business environment.

In addition to networking and professional development, embracing cultural norms and etiquette is essential for effective communication and collaboration in a cross-cultural setting. Understanding and appreciating French business customs, greetings, and communication styles can foster positive relationships with colleagues and clients.

Mentorship can also play a valuable role in an expatriate's professional development journey. Seeking guidance from experienced professionals or industry experts can provide valuable insights and help expatriates navigate the nuances of the French business landscape.

In conclusion, Section 5 emphasizes the importance of networking and professional development for expatriates in France. Engaging in networking events and online platforms enables expatriates to expand their professional connections and gain visibility in the local business community. Investing in continuous learning and skill enhancement is essential for career advancement and staying competitive in the job market. By embracing networking opportunities, professional development initiatives, and cultural understanding, expatriates can thrive in their careers and make a meaningful impact in the diverse and dynamic business landscape of France.

Chapter 6: Learning the Language and Adapting to the Culture

Chapter 6 of this guide focuses on the critical aspects of language learning and cultural adaptation for expatriates in France. Embracing the French language and culture is key to successful integration and making the most of the expatriate experience in this culturally rich and diverse country.

Section 1: Learning the French Language

- Importance of Language Proficiency: Understand the significance of learning the French language for effective communication, social interactions, and professional opportunities in France.

- Language Learning Resources: Explore various language learning resources, including language schools, online courses, language exchange programs, and mobile applications, to help expatriates acquire language skills at their own pace.

- Immersion and Practice: Emphasize the benefits of language immersion through everyday interactions, joining language meet-ups, and seeking opportunities to practice speaking French with native speakers.

Section 2: Embracing French Culture and Etiquette

- Understanding French Culture: Learn about the cultural nuances, customs, and traditions that are integral to French society, including greetings, dining etiquette, and social norms.

- Work Culture and Business Etiquette: Gain insights into the French work culture and business etiquette, such as communication styles, punctuality, and appropriate attire in professional settings.

- Celebrations and Festivals: Familiarize oneself with French celebrations and festivals, such as Bastille Day, Christmas markets, and regional events, to engage in cultural experiences and celebrations.

Section 3: Navigating Daily Life in France

- Local Transportation and Services: Get acquainted with the public transportation system, local services, and amenities available in different regions of France.

- Grocery Shopping and Cuisine: Explore the French culinary delights and learn about grocery shopping, local markets, and dining etiquette to savor the diverse and delicious cuisine of France.

- Healthcare and Services: Understand the healthcare system and access to medical services in France, as well as other essential services that expatriates may require during their stay.

Section 4: Building Relationships and Socializing

- Making Friends and Social Circles: Discover strategies for building friendships and social connections, including joining clubs, sports teams, and community activities.

- Navigating Social Invitations: Learn about French social invitations and customs for accepting or declining invitations to social gatherings.

- Cross-Cultural Communication: Understand effective cross-cultural communication to bridge cultural gaps and foster meaningful relationships with both locals and fellow expatriates.

Section 5: Coping with Culture Shock

- Recognizing Culture Shock: Acknowledge the stages and symptoms of culture shock and strategies for managing its impact on mental well-being.

- Seeking Support: Explore resources for seeking support and overcoming challenges related to cultural adaptation, including local expatriate communities, counseling services, and support groups.

In conclusion, Chapter 6 highlights the significance of language learning and cultural adaptation for expatriates in France. Mastering the French language facilitates seamless communication and enhances social and professional integration. Embracing French culture, customs, and etiquette enriches the expatriate experience and fosters meaningful connections with the local community. Navigating daily life, building relationships, and coping with culture shock are essential aspects of successful cultural adaptation. By immersing themselves in the language and culture of France, expatriates can embrace the diversity and charm of the country, making their stay more rewarding and fulfilling.

1. Learning the French Language

In Section 1 of this guide, we emphasize the importance of learning the French language for expatriates in France. Acquiring proficiency in French is not only crucial for effective communication but also an essential step towards cultural integration and successful adaptation to life in the country.

Learning the French language opens doors to various opportunities, both socially and professionally. While English is widely spoken, particularly in urban areas and within international business circles, French remains the primary language of communication for most daily interactions. Having a solid grasp of French allows expatriates to engage in meaningful conversations with locals, participate in cultural events, and establish meaningful connections in their communities.

Numerous language learning resources are available to expatriates, catering to different learning preferences and schedules. Language schools and private tutors offer structured courses with personalized guidance, ensuring learners can progress at their own pace. Online language platforms and mobile applications provide convenient and flexible options for self-directed learning, with interactive exercises and multimedia content to enhance language skills.

Language immersion is a powerful tool for language acquisition. Engaging in everyday interactions in French, such as ordering at a local café or striking up conversations with neighbors, allows expatriates to practice their language skills in real-life situations. Joining language exchange programs or language meet-ups also provides opportunities to

practice speaking with native French speakers and other language learners, creating a supportive and motivating learning environment.

The benefits of learning the French language extend beyond practical communication. Language proficiency fosters a deeper understanding and appreciation of French culture, literature, and history. It allows
expatriates to engage more fully in French society, participate in cultural traditions and celebrations, and build stronger connections with locals.

Language learning requires dedication and consistent effort, but
the rewards are invaluable. Expatriates who embrace the journey of language acquisition find that it enriches their experience in France and
facilitates smoother integration into the local community. Overcoming
the language barrier opens doors to a deeper sense of belonging and enhances the overall expatriate experience in this culturally vibrant and
diverse country.

2. Embracing French Culture and Etiquette

In Section 2 of this guide, we delve into the significance of embracing
French culture and etiquette for expatriates living in France. Understanding and appreciating French customs and traditions are essential
for building meaningful connections with the local community and
navigating social and professional interactions with ease.

French culture is deeply rooted in history, arts, and gastronomy,
and it plays a central role in the daily lives of its residents. Expatriates
can start by familiarizing themselves with common greetings and expressions used in social interactions. The French value politeness, so
saying "Bonjour" (good morning) or "Bonsoir" (good evening) upon
entering a shop or any public space is considered polite and respectful.

Dining etiquette is an integral part of French culture. The French
take great pride in their cuisine and culinary traditions. Understanding
table manners, such as keeping one's hands on the table and resting the
wrists on the edge, can help expatriates feel more at ease during meals.

Taking the time to savor each course and embracing the leisurely-paced dining experience is also a hallmark of French meals.

Work culture and business etiquette in France may differ from what expatriates are accustomed to in their home countries. French business interactions often prioritize building personal relationships before discussing business matters. Addressing colleagues and superiors using appropriate titles, such as "Monsieur" (Mr.) or "Madame" (Mrs.), is customary and demonstrates respect in professional settings.

French society places significant value on cultural celebrations and festivals. Expatriates can immerse themselves in these cultural events to gain a deeper understanding of French traditions. Participating in local celebrations like Bastille Day (July 14th), Christmas markets, and regional festivals can be enriching experiences that bring expatriates closer to the heart of French culture.

Taking the time to learn basic French phrases and expressions can go a long way in demonstrating respect for the local culture. Even if expatriates are not yet fluent, making an effort to communicate in French, even with some mistakes, is often appreciated by locals and can lead to warmer interactions.

Building relationships with French locals and fellow expatriates is an essential part of embracing French culture. Joining clubs, sports teams, or community organizations can create opportunities for socializing and making friends. Engaging in cross-cultural communication with an open mind and a willingness to learn from each other fosters mutual understanding and fosters harmonious relationships.

In conclusion, Section 2 highlights the significance of embracing French culture and etiquette for expatriates living in France. Understanding common greetings, dining etiquette, and social customs contributes to smoother interactions and integration into the local community. Embracing cultural celebrations and festivals enriches the expatriate experience and creates opportunities for meaningful cultural exchange. By immersing themselves in French culture with an open and respectful mindset, expatriates can forge deeper connections and fully appreciate the beauty and richness of this captivating country.

3. Navigating Daily Life in France

Section 3 of this guide focuses on the practical aspects of navigating daily life for expatriates in France. Understanding local transportation, accessing essential services, and embracing the culinary delights are essential for a smooth and enjoyable expatriate experience.

Public transportation is an integral part of daily life in France, offering efficient and extensive networks in major cities and regions. Expatriates can benefit from various transportation options, including buses, trams, and metro systems. Investing in a rechargeable transportation card, such as Navigo in Paris or similar cards in other cities, allows for seamless travel within urban areas and reduces commuting expenses.

French cuisine is renowned worldwide, and expatriates have the opportunity to indulge in a diverse range of culinary delights. Local markets offer fresh produce, cheeses, and pastries that reflect the flavors of different regions. Embracing French dining customs, such as enjoying leisurely meals and appreciating each course, is an integral part of the gastronomic experience.

Grocery shopping in France can be a delightful adventure as well. Supermarkets and hypermarkets offer a wide selection of products, and specialty shops cater to specific culinary preferences. Locals often take pride in their regional specialties, and expatriates can explore various French delicacies during their stay.

Navigating essential services is vital for a comfortable daily life. France boasts a robust healthcare system with access to quality medical care. Expatriates should familiarize themselves with their local healthcare facilities, register with a general practitioner, and ensure they have the necessary health insurance coverage.

Furthermore, understanding the administrative procedures for essential services can be beneficial. Setting up utilities like electricity, gas, and internet often requires contacting service providers and providing necessary documentation. Many administrative tasks can be completed online, simplifying the process for expatriates.

Expatriates should be aware of local customs related to tipping, greeting, and social interactions. In France, a modest tip is often appreciated for good service in restaurants, cafes, or taxis. Handshakes are common for greetings in professional settings, while kisses on the cheeks are customary among acquaintances in social situations.

France's diverse regions offer unique landscapes and cultural experiences. Each area has its charm, traditions, and local events, contributing to the country's rich tapestry. Exploring the local attractions and participating in regional festivities can provide a deeper appreciation of France's cultural diversity.

In conclusion, Section 3 provides expatriates with practical guidance on navigating daily life in France. Efficient public transportation, access to quality healthcare, and a world-renowned culinary scene contribute to a comfortable and fulfilling experience. Understanding local customs and embracing regional traditions enhance social interactions and promote meaningful cultural exchange. By immersing themselves in daily life in France, expatriates can fully appreciate the beauty and allure of this captivating country.

4. Building Relationships and Socializing

In Section 4 of this guide, we explore the significance of building relationships and socializing for expatriates in France. Establishing meaningful connections with both locals and fellow expatriates is essential for a fulfilling and enriching expatriate experience.

Building relationships with French locals can be facilitated through various channels. Joining clubs, sports teams, or community organizations provides opportunities for expatriates to engage with like-minded individuals and participate in shared interests. Volunteering for local causes and community events not only contributes positively to the community but also fosters connections with locals who share similar values and passions.

Language exchange programs and language meet-ups are excellent platforms for expatriates to practice their French language skills while connecting with native speakers. Engaging in conversations with locals allows expatriates to learn more about French culture, customs, and daily life from an authentic perspective.

Socializing with fellow expatriates can also play a vital role in creating a supportive community abroad. Expatriate groups and online forums offer platforms for expatriates to share experiences, seek advice, and organize social gatherings. Attending expatriate-oriented events and meet-ups can provide a sense of camaraderie and help expatriates adapt to their new environment more smoothly.

French culture places a strong emphasis on leisure and enjoying quality time with friends and family. Invitations to social gatherings, such as dinner parties or picnics, are common in French society. Accepting these invitations and participating in social events present opportunities for expatriates to build friendships and integrate into the local community.

Cross-cultural communication plays a crucial role in building relationships and socializing. Being open-minded, respectful, and sensitive to cultural differences fosters positive interactions. Learning about French customs for greetings, gift-giving, and other social norms helps expatriates navigate social situations with ease and understanding.

Participating in local celebrations and festivals is an excellent way to immerse oneself in French culture and create lasting memories. French festivals, such as Bastille Day, Fête de la Musique, or local Carnivals, provide expatriates with unique cultural experiences and opportunities to celebrate alongside the local community.

In conclusion, Section 4 emphasizes the importance of building relationships and socializing for expatriates in France. Engaging with locals and fellow expatriates through various activities and events creates a supportive and enriching social network. By embracing cross-cultural communication and participating in French traditions and celebrations, expatriates can forge meaningful connections and fully immerse themselves in the vibrant and diverse social fabric of France. Establishing a strong sense of community enhances the expatriate experience and contributes to a rewarding stay in this captivating country.

5. Coping with Culture Shock

In Section 5 of this guide, we address the phenomenon of culture shock and provide strategies for expatriates to cope with the challenges that may arise during their transition to life in France. Culture shock is a common experience when relocating to a new country, and understanding its stages and symptoms is essential for managing its impact on mental well-being.

Culture shock typically occurs in four stages: the honeymoon stage, the frustration stage, the adjustment stage, and the acceptance stage. During the honeymoon stage, everything about the new environment may seem exciting and enchanting. However, as the novelty wears off, expatriates may enter the frustration stage, where cultural differences, language barriers, and homesickness can lead to feelings of disorientation and discomfort.

The adjustment stage marks a turning point, where expatriates begin to adapt to the new culture and develop coping mechanisms. It is crucial to remain patient with oneself during this phase, as adaptation takes time. Eventually, expatriates reach the acceptance stage, where they become more at ease with the new culture and feel a sense of belonging in their adopted home.

To cope with culture shock effectively, seeking support and staying connected with others are paramount. Engaging with local expatriate communities or support groups allows individuals to share experiences and emotions with people who understand the challenges of living abroad. Support networks provide valuable advice and encouragement, making the adjustment process feel less daunting.

Maintaining communication with family and friends back home can also help expatriates manage homesickness and feelings of isolation. Video calls, emails, and social media platforms enable expatriates to stay connected to their loved ones and provide a sense of continuity amidst the changes in their lives.

Participating in activities and hobbies that bring joy and comfort can help alleviate the stress of culture shock. Exploring familiar pastimes or discovering new interests can offer a sense of normalcy and a source of pleasure during challenging times.

Engaging in mindfulness practices, such as meditation or yoga, can promote emotional well-being and reduce stress. Taking time for self-care and relaxation is essential for maintaining a positive mindset and adapting to the cultural shifts.

Learning about French culture, history, and traditions can foster appreciation and understanding of the host country, helping expatriates to embrace their new surroundings. Gaining knowledge about the local customs and norms can also help mitigate misunderstandings and enhance cultural awareness.

Lastly, seeking professional support through counseling or therapy can be beneficial for expatriates experiencing significant emotional difficulties during their transition. Professional counselors or psychologists can offer guidance and strategies for coping with culture shock and managing the emotional challenges that may arise.

In conclusion, Section 5 provides expatriates with strategies for coping with culture shock during their stay in France. Understanding the stages of culture shock and seeking support from expatriate communities and loved ones are crucial aspects of managing the adjustment process. Engaging in self-care, staying connected, and learning about the local culture all contribute to a smoother adaptation to the new environment. By proactively addressing culture shock, expatriates can navigate their expatriate journey with resilience and openness, making the most of their experience in this captivating and culturally rich country.

Chapter 7: Transportation and Getting Around

Chapter 7 of this guide focuses on transportation and navigating the various means of getting around in France. Whether in bustling cities or picturesque countryside, understanding the transportation options is essential for expatriates to explore the country conveniently and efficiently.

Section 1: Public Transportation in Cities

- Overview of Public Transportation: Explores the well-developed public transportation systems in major French cities, including metros, trams, buses, and RER (Réseau Express Régional) trains.

- Ticketing and Passes: Provides information on ticketing options, such as single-journey tickets, day passes, and monthly or annual transportation cards for frequent commuters.

- Navigating Public Transportation: Offers practical tips on reading maps, using ticket machines, and planning routes using online apps or transport websites.

Section 2: Intercity Travel by Train

- High-Speed Trains (TGV): Highlights the TGV network, renowned for its speed and efficiency, connecting major cities across France and neighboring countries.

- Regional Trains (TER): Explores the extensive network of regional trains, allowing expatriates to explore picturesque towns and scenic routes.

- Booking Train Tickets: Provides guidance on booking train tickets through official websites or train stations, along with different fare options and discounts available.

Section 3: Driving in France

- Driver's License and International Driving Permit: Clarifies the requirements for driving in France with a foreign driver's license and the need for an International Driving Permit.

- Road Rules and Traffic Regulations: Familiarizes expatriates with French road rules, speed limits, and parking regulations to ensure safe driving experiences.

- Renting a Car: Offers insights into the process of renting a car in France, including popular rental companies and documentation needed.

Section 4: Cycling and Walking

- Bicycle-Friendly Cities: Highlights the bicycle-friendly cities and bike-sharing programs available in various urban areas.

- Pedestrian-Friendly Zones: Explores pedestrian-friendly zones and city centers designed for walking and strolling, encouraging eco-friendly transportation.

Section 5: Air Travel and International Connections

- Airports in France: Provides an overview of major international airports in France, including Paris Charles de Gaulle Airport and Paris Orly Airport.

- Domestic Flights: Explores the availability of domestic flights connecting major cities and regional airports within the country.

- International Connections: Offers information on connecting flights to other European and international destinations.

In conclusion, Chapter 7 equips expatriates with comprehensive knowledge about transportation and getting around in France. Understanding the public transportation systems, intercity trains, driving regulations, and alternative modes of transportation empowers expatriates to explore the diverse landscapes, vibrant cities, and charming regions of this captivating country. By utilizing the various transportation options available, expatriates can make the most of their time in France and embark on memorable journeys throughout this culturally rich and picturesque nation.

1. Public Transportation in Cities

Section 1 of this guide provides an overview of the efficient and extensive public transportation systems available in major cities across France. Public transportation is a popular and eco-friendly option for getting around urban areas, offering convenience and accessibility to residents and expatriates alike.

In major cities like Paris, Lyon, Marseille, and Bordeaux, the public transportation networks consist of metros, trams, buses, and RER (Réseau Express Régional) trains. The metro systems, known for their efficiency and frequency, are the backbone of urban transportation, connecting various neighborhoods and landmarks within the cities. Trams complement the metro system, offering additional connectivity to specific areas with a focus on sustainability and reduced emissions.

Buses serve as a vital mode of public transportation, covering routes not accessible by the metro or tram lines. They are particularly useful for reaching neighborhoods further away from the city center or for late-night journeys when other services may have limited operating hours. Buses in major cities are often equipped with real-time tracking systems, making it easy for passengers to know when the next bus will arrive.

The RER trains are a part of the regional transportation system, providing fast connections between the city center and nearby suburbs or satellite towns. RER trains are especially valuable for commuters traveling longer distances to work or for those exploring areas beyond the city limits.

Public transportation ticketing is designed to accommodate various needs and travel frequencies. Options include single-journey tickets, day passes, and weekly or monthly transportation cards. For frequent commuters, purchasing monthly or annual passes can be cost-effective and practical.

Navigating the public transportation system is made easier with clear signage, maps, and announcements in multiple languages, including English. Many cities have user-friendly mobile apps and websites that provide real-time updates on schedules, delays, and route planning. These apps also help expatriates access essential information, such as fare prices and nearby stations.

Using public transportation in cities offers several advantages, including cost-effectiveness, reduced carbon footprint, and avoidance of traffic congestion. It also allows expatriates to immerse themselves in the local culture and experience city life like a resident.

In conclusion, Section 1 highlights the efficiency and convenience of public transportation in major cities across France. The well-developed metro, tram, bus, and RER systems provide reliable connectivity and accessibility, making it easy for expatriates to navigate urban areas. By utilizing the public transportation options available, expatriates can efficiently explore city landmarks, cultural hotspots, and hidden gems while embracing the vibrant lifestyle of French cities.

2. Intercity Travel by Train

Section 2 of this guide focuses on intercity travel by train, one of the most efficient and enjoyable ways to explore the diverse regions of France. The country's extensive and reliable train network connects major cities, picturesque towns, and scenic countryside, offering expatriates a seamless and memorable travel experience.

The TGV (Train à Grande Vitesse) is the pride of France's train system, known for its high-speed capabilities and efficiency. TGV trains connect major cities like Paris, Lyon, Marseille, Bordeaux, and many others, covering long distances in a fraction of the time it would take by road. Traveling at speeds of up to 320 km/h (200 mph), the TGV allows expatriates to conveniently visit various regions, making day trips or weekend getaways a viable option.

Beyond the TGV, France's regional train network, known as TER (Transport Express Régional), extends its reach to less populated areas, connecting smaller towns and rural destinations. Traveling by TER allows expatriates to immerse themselves in the picturesque landscapes of the French countryside, exploring charming villages and historic sites off the beaten path.

Booking train tickets is a straightforward process, with various options available to suit different travel preferences. Expatriates can book tickets in advance through official websites or at train stations. France offers a range of fare options, including discounted fares for early booking or youth, and the SNCF (Société Nationale des Chemins de fer Français) often announces special promotions throughout the year.

For longer journeys or frequent travelers, the SNCF offers loyalty programs like "Voyageur" that provide additional benefits and rewards. Travelers can accumulate points and enjoy perks such as free tickets or access to business lounges at train stations.

During the journey, passengers can expect a comfortable and well-equipped train experience. TGV trains offer spacious seating, power outlets, and complimentary Wi-Fi, allowing travelers to stay connected throughout their journey. TER trains provide a more intimate setting, often offering panoramic windows that showcase the beauty of the French countryside.

Intercity travel by train not only provides convenience and efficiency but also allows expatriates to experience the essence of French culture and hospitality. Train stations often showcase local architecture and regional specialties, providing an introduction to the unique character of each destination.

In conclusion, Section 2 highlights the convenience and charm of intercity travel by train in France. The TGV and TER networks offer expatriates a fast, reliable, and scenic mode of transportation, connecting them to iconic cities, charming towns, and breathtaking landscapes. By embarking on train journeys, expatriates can embark on unforgettable adventures, immersing themselves in the rich history, culture, and beauty that France has to offer.

3. Driving in France

Section 3 of this guide provides valuable insights into driving in France, offering expatriates essential information to navigate the roadways safely and efficiently. Whether exploring the countryside or commuting within cities, understanding the rules and regulations is crucial for a smooth driving experience.

Expatriates planning to drive in France should ensure that they have a valid driver's license from their home country. For those staying in France for an extended period, it is advisable to obtain an International Driving Permit (IDP) in addition to their local license. The IDP serves as a translation of the driver's license and is recognized by French authorities.

French road rules and traffic regulations are similar to those in many other European countries. Speed limits, for instance, vary depending on the type of road and location. Speed limits are typically posted, with 50 km/h (31 mph) in urban areas, 80 km/h (50 mph) on secondary roads, and 130 km/h (81 mph) on highways.

Seat belts are mandatory for all passengers, and children under ten years old are required to sit in an appropriate child safety seat. Using a mobile phone while driving is strictly prohibited unless in hands-free mode.

In urban areas, expatriates may encounter roundabouts, which are common in France. Understanding the rules for navigating roundabouts, such as giving way to vehicles already in the circle, is essential for safe driving.

Parking regulations in French cities can vary, with different colored parking zones indicating different rules. In central areas, parking spaces may be limited, so using public transportation or designated parking lots is often more convenient.

For expatriates who prefer the convenience of driving but do not own a car, rental car services are readily available throughout France. Major cities and airports offer rental options from well-known international companies, making it easy to access a vehicle for day trips or weekend getaways.

Driving in rural areas of France offers picturesque routes through charming villages and stunning landscapes. However, expatriates should be mindful of narrow roads, especially in older towns, and watch for pedestrians and cyclists, who share the road.

In conclusion, Section 3 provides expatriates with comprehensive information about driving in France. Understanding the rules and regulations, as well as road signs and traffic norms, is essential for safe and enjoyable driving experiences. Whether exploring the countryside or navigating through bustling cities, driving in France offers the freedom to discover the country's beauty and diversity at one's own pace. By adhering to the road rules and driving responsibly, expatriates can embark on unforgettable road trips and fully embrace the enchanting landscapes and cultural treasures that France has to offer.

4. Cycling and Walking

Section 4 of this guide delves into the delightful options of cycling and walking in France, which offer unique and eco-friendly ways to explore the country's urban centers and picturesque landscapes. Both cycling and walking are popular modes of transportation and leisure activities for residents and expatriates alike, providing opportunities to experience the charm of France at a leisurely pace.

Many French cities have embraced cycling as a sustainable means of transportation. Urban centers are equipped with bike lanes and bike-sharing programs, making it easy for expatriates to rent bicycles for short journeys or sightseeing tours. Cycling offers an intimate and immersive experience, allowing travelers to discover hidden alleys, scenic riverbanks, and iconic landmarks while enjoying the fresh air and picturesque surroundings. Additionally, cycling is a fantastic way to stay active and healthy while exploring the cities' cultural hotspots.

For those who prefer walking, France's pedestrian-friendly zones and historic city centers are a treat to explore. Cities like Paris, Strasbourg, and Avignon boast captivating old-world architecture and charming streets that invite leisurely strolls. Walking tours are popular in various cities, led by knowledgeable guides who share fascinating insights into the local history, art, and culture.

Beyond the urban centers, France offers stunning landscapes that are best appreciated on foot or by bike. The French countryside boasts a network of scenic hiking trails that lead to rolling vineyards, rugged coastlines, and breathtaking mountain vistas. The Camino de Santiago, a historic pilgrimage route, also passes through parts of France, providing a unique and spiritual trekking experience.

Cycling and walking not only allow expatriates to connect with nature and immerse themselves in the local ambiance but also offer eco-friendly and sustainable ways to travel. Choosing these modes of transportation contributes to reducing carbon emissions and aligns with France's commitment to environmental conservation.

Safety is a top priority for cyclists and pedestrians in France. Cyclists are required to wear helmets when riding on highways and busy roads, and bike lights are mandatory during low-light conditions. Pedestrians should use designated crosswalks and pedestrian crossings for safe road crossings.

In conclusion, Section 4 highlights the pleasures of cycling and walking in France. These eco-friendly and immersive modes of transportation provide expatriates with unique opportunities to explore the country's diverse landscapes, historic cities, and enchanting countryside. Whether cycling through urban centers or embarking on scenic hikes, expatriates can fully appreciate the beauty and cultural richness that France has to offer. By embracing these sustainable and leisurely travel options, expatriates can forge lasting memories and discover the hidden gems of this captivating country.

5. Air Travel and International Connections

Section 5 of this guide delves into air travel and international connections in France, providing expatriates with valuable information about the country's airports, domestic flights, and international connectivity. With a well-developed aviation infrastructure, France offers convenient and efficient options for both domestic and international travel.

France is home to several major international airports, with Paris Charles de Gaulle Airport being one of the busiest and most significant aviation hubs in Europe. As the primary gateway to the country, this airport serves as a vital link connecting France to destinations worldwide. Paris Orly Airport is another major airport in the capital, providing additional international and domestic flight options.

Beyond Paris, other major cities such as Lyon, Marseille, Nice, and Bordeaux also boast international airports with direct flights to various destinations. These regional airports offer convenient options for expatriates located outside of the capital.

For domestic travel within France, expatriates have the option to fly to different regions using domestic flights. Several airlines operate domestic routes, providing quick and efficient connections between major cities and smaller towns. Domestic flights are particularly beneficial when covering long distances, such as from Paris to the south of France or from one end of the country to the other.

France's central location in Europe makes it a prime destination for international connections. Paris, in particular, serves as a major hub for intercontinental flights, making it easy for expatriates to reach destinations beyond Europe. With multiple airlines operating in and out of France, expatriates have a wide array of choices for planning international trips.

For frequent travelers, loyalty programs offered by airlines can provide significant benefits. By accumulating points through travel, expatriates can enjoy perks such as priority boarding, lounge access, and complimentary upgrades, making air travel a more comfortable and enjoyable experience.

Expatriates planning international travel from France should familiarize themselves with customs and immigration regulations. Knowing the necessary documentation, visa requirements, and customs restrictions for their destination countries is essential to avoid any travel complications.

In conclusion, Section 5 emphasizes the convenience and connectivity of air travel in France. The country's major international airports, regional airports, and extensive domestic flight options make traveling within France and to international destinations efficient and accessible. By utilizing the well-established aviation infrastructure, expatriates can easily explore France's diverse regions and embark on unforgettable journeys to destinations beyond its borders. Whether for business or leisure, air travel provides expatriates with a seamless and enjoyable means of reaching their desired destinations.

Chapter 8: Making Friends and Building a Social Life

Chapter 8 of this guide focuses on the importance of making friends and building a social life for expatriates living in France. Establishing meaningful connections with both locals and fellow expatriates is vital for a fulfilling and enriching expatriate experience. This chapter offers valuable insights and practical tips to help expatriates forge friendships, find social activities, and create a supportive social network in their new home.

Section 1: Engaging with Local Communities

- Embracing French Culture: Encourages expatriates to participate in local cultural events, festivals, and celebrations, which provide opportunities to meet locals and immerse themselves in French traditions.

- Learning the Language: Highlights the importance of learning French as a means to better connect with the local community, understand cultural nuances, and engage in more meaningful conversations.

Section 2: Joining Expat Communities and Groups

- Utilizing Expat Networks: Explores the benefits of joining expatriate communities and groups, where expatriates can find support, share experiences, and engage in social activities with like-minded individuals from various backgrounds.

- Attending Expat Events: Recommends attending expat-oriented events, social gatherings, and meet-ups organized by expatriate associations or online platforms, which provide an excellent opportunity to make friends and expand social circles.

Section 3: Participating in Social Activities and Hobbies

- Exploring Shared Interests: Encourages expatriates to pursue their hobbies and passions, such as sports, art, cooking, or music, and join clubs or classes where they can meet people with similar interests.

- Engaging in Recreational Activities: Suggests participating in recreational activities, such as hiking, cycling, or sports clubs, as a way to meet active and adventurous individuals and create lasting connections.

Section 4: Volunteering and Community Involvement

- Contributing to the Community: Highlights the value of volunteering for local causes, community projects, or charity organizations, which not only benefits the community but also provides opportunities to meet like-minded individuals with a shared sense of purpose.

- Building Bonds through Giving: Volunteering fosters meaningful connections and friendships based on shared values and a desire to make a positive impact on society.

Section 5: Leveraging Online Social Platforms

- Utilizing Social Media: Explores the role of social media platforms and online forums in connecting expatriates, providing a virtual space to exchange information, seek advice, and organize social gatherings.

- Joining Expatriate Groups: Recommends joining online expatriate groups on platforms like Facebook or Meetup, where expatriates can interact, ask questions, and find local events.

In conclusion, Chapter 8 emphasizes the significance of making friends and building a social life for expatriates in France. Engaging with local communities, joining expatriate networks, participating in social activities, and leveraging online platforms all contribute to creating a supportive and fulfilling social life abroad. By proactively seeking opportunities to connect with others and embrace the culture and traditions of France, expatriates can forge meaningful friendships and build a strong social network that enriches their expatriate journey and enhances their overall experience in this captivating and culturally diverse country.

1. Engaging with Local Communities

Section 1 of this guide emphasizes the importance of engaging with local communities for expatriates living in France. Building connections with the local population not only enriches the expatriate experience but also fosters a deeper understanding and appreciation of the country's culture and way of life.

Embracing French culture is a pivotal step in connecting with the local community. Participating in cultural events, festivals, and celebrations allows expatriates to experience firsthand the traditions, customs, and values that are integral to French society. Attending events like Bastille Day parades, local music festivals, or regional culinary fairs provides opportunities to interact with locals, creating shared experiences that form the foundation for meaningful friendships.

Learning the French language is essential for effective communication and integration into the local community. While many French citizens speak English and are accommodating to non-native speakers, making an effort to speak the local language demonstrates respect for the culture and opens doors to more authentic and profound interactions. Enrolling in language classes or language exchange programs can facilitate language learning and provide a supportive environment to practice conversational skills.

Beyond language and cultural events, expatriates can also engage with the local community through volunteer work and community involvement. Volunteering for local causes or participating in community projects enables expatriates to give back to society and build bonds with like-minded individuals who share a passion for making a positive impact.

Additionally, joining local clubs, sports teams, or hobby groups centered around shared interests can provide expatriates with a sense of belonging and camaraderie. Whether it's joining a local football club, an art workshop, or a book club, these activities offer opportunities to meet individuals who share similar passions and forge friendships beyond language and cultural barriers.

Engaging with local communities not only enhances the expatriate's social life but also provides a deeper connection to the place they now call home. Establishing authentic relationships with locals helps dispel the feeling of being an outsider and contributes to a more fulfilling and integrated experience in France.

In conclusion, Section 1 underscores the significance of engaging with local communities for expatriates in France. Embracing French culture, learning the language, and participating in local events facilitate connections with locals and create opportunities for meaningful social interactions. By immersing themselves in the local community, expatriates can forge lasting friendships and gain a profound appreciation for the rich tapestry of French culture and society. Building bridges with the local population paves the way for a rewarding and truly immersive expatriate journey in this captivating and culturally vibrant country.

2. Joining Expat Communities and Groups

Section 2 of this guide highlights the value of joining expatriate communities and groups as a means for expatriates in France to find support, camaraderie, and social opportunities with individuals who share similar international experiences and backgrounds.

Expatriate communities play a vital role in providing a sense of belonging for those living far from their home countries. These communities often consist of diverse individuals from various nationalities, making them a melting pot of cultures, languages, and perspectives. By participating in expat-oriented events and gatherings, expatriates can connect with like-minded individuals who understand the joys and challenges of living abroad.

Joining expatriate groups and associations also offers practical benefits, such as access to valuable information and advice. Expatriates can seek guidance on navigating bureaucratic processes, finding essential services, and adjusting to life in a new country from those who have gone through similar experiences.

Social events organized by expatriate groups create opportunities for expatriates to meet new people, expand their social circles, and forge friendships beyond their immediate surroundings. Events like cultural exchanges, international dinners, and language exchange meet-ups encourage interactions between individuals from diverse backgrounds, fostering a global community spirit.

Additionally, joining expatriate groups can ease the transition into a new environment by providing a safety net of support. Expatriates can rely on fellow members for practical help, emotional support, and even practical assistance in settling into their new homes.

Expatriate communities in France are often inclusive and welcoming to new members. Many groups maintain online forums or social media platforms where expatriates can connect virtually before arriving in the country, making the integration process smoother and less daunting.

While engaging with local communities is essential for cultural immersion, expatriate groups serve as a comforting bridge between the familiar and the unfamiliar. They provide a sense of home away from home, making the adjustment to a new country more manageable and enjoyable.

In conclusion, Section 2 emphasizes the significance of joining expatriate communities and groups for expatriates in France. These groups offer a sense of camaraderie, support, and friendship among individuals who share similar international experiences. By participating in expat-oriented events and gatherings, expatriates can build a global network of friends, access valuable information, and ease their transition into the French way of life. Embracing both local communities and expatriate groups enriches the expatriate journey, creating a fulfilling and interconnected experience in this diverse and welcoming country.

3. Participating in Social Activities and Hobbies

Section 3 of this guide encourages expatriates in France to participate in social activities and pursue hobbies as a means to connect with others, engage in meaningful interactions, and enrich their social life. Engaging in social activities and hobbies provides expatriates with opportunities to explore their interests, bond with like-minded individuals, and create lasting friendships, ultimately enhancing their overall expatriate experience.

Exploring shared interests is a fantastic way for expatriates to find common ground with others and build connections. Whether it's sports, arts, music, cooking, or dance, joining clubs or classes related to their passions enables expatriates to meet people who share their enthusiasm. These social environments offer a relaxed and enjoyable setting for interacting with others and offer an organic platform for forming friendships.

Participating in recreational activities is another excellent way for expatriates to engage socially and embrace the local lifestyle. France offers a diverse range of outdoor activities such as hiking, cycling, and water sports in its picturesque landscapes. Joining outdoor activity groups or organized tours not only allows expatriates to explore the natural beauty of their new home but also facilitates interactions with fellow nature enthusiasts and outdoor adventurers.

Attending social events and gatherings hosted by local communities, expatriate groups, or social clubs can be an enriching experience for expatriates seeking to expand their social circles. These events provide a welcoming atmosphere for meeting new people, fostering cultural exchanges, and learning about different perspectives and traditions.

International dinners, language exchange meet-ups, and themed social nights are some examples of events that encourage connections and create a sense of community.

Pursuing hobbies and participating in social activities also promotes personal well-being and mental health. Engaging in activities that bring joy and fulfillment can reduce stress and provide a sense of accomplishment. This positive mindset can enhance social interactions, making expatriates more approachable and receptive to building connections with others.

Moreover, exploring social activities and hobbies helps expatriates step out of their comfort zones and embrace new experiences. Trying something new allows them to grow personally and culturally, fostering a sense of adaptability and openness to the diversity of life in France.

In conclusion, Section 3 highlights the significance of participating in social activities and hobbies for expatriates in France. Engaging in shared interests, recreational pursuits, and social events provides expatriates with avenues to meet like-minded individuals, form friendships, and embrace the cultural diversity of their new home. Pursuing hobbies not only enriches the expatriate experience but also contributes to personal growth and well-being. By actively engaging in social activities, expatriates can create a vibrant and fulfilling social life that enhances their overall enjoyment of living in this captivating and culturally rich country.

4. Volunteering and Community Involvement

Section 4 of this guide emphasizes the significance of volunteering and community involvement for expatriates in France. Engaging in volunteer work not only allows expatriates to contribute positively to society but also creates meaningful opportunities to connect with locals, fellow expatriates, and other like-minded individuals who share a sense of social responsibility.

Volunteering is an excellent way for expatriates to give back to their new community and make a positive impact on the lives of others. Whether it's participating in local environmental initiatives, assisting at community centers, or volunteering for charitable organizations, expatriates can play a role in addressing societal needs and contributing to the greater good.

By engaging in volunteer activities, expatriates have the chance to meet locals and interact with people from various walks of life. Working side by side on common causes creates a shared sense of purpose and fosters connections beyond language and cultural barriers. These interactions offer invaluable insights into the local culture, customs, and values, promoting a deeper understanding of the community in which they reside.

Volunteering also allows expatriates to build strong bonds with fellow volunteers, both local and international. Shared experiences and joint efforts in making a positive impact create a sense of camaraderie and friendship. The friendships formed through volunteering can become a valuable support system, especially for those who are far away from their original support networks.

In addition to social benefits, volunteering can help expatriates develop new skills, gain professional experience, and enhance their resume. Many volunteer positions involve teamwork, leadership, problem-solving, and communication, which are transferable skills highly valued in various fields.

Community involvement extends beyond formal volunteering and can include engaging with local events, supporting neighborhood initiatives, and participating in local cultural activities. Expatriates can attend local festivals, art exhibitions, or town hall meetings to immerse themselves in the community's rhythm and stay informed about local affairs.

To explore volunteer opportunities, expatriates can reach out to local charities, community centers, and international organizations operating in France. Online platforms and social media groups dedicated to volunteering can also provide valuable information on ongoing projects and initiatives seeking volunteer support.

In conclusion, Section 4 underscores the importance of volunteering and community involvement for expatriates in France. Engaging in volunteer work provides expatriates with a chance to give back, connect with the local community, and develop meaningful friendships with fellow volunteers. Participating in community events and cultural activities further strengthens the bond with the local community and enriches the expatriate experience. By being actively involved in their new surroundings, expatriates can make a positive impact while embracing the values of empathy, collaboration, and social responsibility that are integral to French society.

5. Leveraging Online Social Platforms

Section 5 of this guide explores the significance of leveraging online social platforms as a valuable tool for expatriates in France to connect with others, find like-minded individuals, and access essential information about their new home.

Social media platforms play a vital role in connecting expatriates with the larger international community residing in France. Joining expatriate groups on platforms like Facebook, Meetup, or InterNations provides a virtual space for expatriates to interact, share experiences, seek advice, and organize social gatherings. These online communities offer a sense of belonging and understanding, as members can relate to the challenges and joys of living abroad.

Online social platforms also facilitate pre-arrival connections. Expatriates can engage with others planning to move to France, allowing them to build friendships and support networks even before arriving in the country. Such virtual connections can ease the transition and provide a welcoming environment upon arrival.

Beyond expatriate groups, various online forums and websites cater to specific interests and hobbies, such as sports, arts, language exchange, and cultural events. Joining these niche communities allows expatriates to discover local events, meet people with shared passions, and participate in activities that align with their interests.

Moreover, online platforms are an excellent resource for accessing essential information about life in France. Expatriate blogs, forums, and websites offer practical tips on navigating bureaucratic processes, finding accommodation, understanding healthcare systems, and dealing with cultural nuances. These resources can be invaluable for expatriates seeking guidance and support during their transition to a new country.

Video conferencing tools and messaging apps further enhance online social connections. Expatriates can stay in touch with family and friends back home and host virtual gatherings with loved ones across borders. These technologies bridge the gap between distances, making the expatriate journey more manageable and less isolating.

As with any online platform, expatriates should exercise caution and privacy when sharing personal information. Keeping online interactions positive and respectful fosters a supportive and welcoming digital community for all members.

In conclusion, Section 5 highlights the importance of leveraging online social platforms for expatriates in France. Joining expatriate groups, engaging in niche communities, and accessing valuable information online fosters connections and eases the transition to a new country. Virtual social connections complement in-person interactions, providing expatriates with a diverse and inclusive support system. By actively participating in online social platforms, expatriates can embrace the power of technology to build friendships, seek advice, and stay connected with their global network while living in this vibrant and culturally rich country.

Chapter 9: Exploring French Culture and Leisure Activities

Chapter 9 of this guide delves into the diverse and enriching aspects of French culture and leisure activities available to expatriates in France. From art and history to culinary delights and outdoor pursuits, this chapter highlights the plethora of opportunities for expatriates to immerse themselves in the captivating essence of French life.

Section 1: Art and History

- Museums and Galleries: Explores renowned art museums like the Louvre, Musée d'Orsay, and Centre Pompidou in Paris, as well as regional museums showcasing local history and culture.

- Historic Landmarks: Discusses iconic landmarks such as the Eiffel Tower, Notre-Dame Cathedral, and the Palace of the Popes in Avignon, which offer a glimpse into France's rich historical heritage.

- Châteaux and Palaces: Highlights the opportunity to visit magnificent châteaux in the Loire Valley and palaces like Versailles, where expatriates can marvel at opulent architecture and lush gardens.

Section 2: Culinary Delights

- Local Cuisine: Explores the diverse regional cuisine of France, from savory crêpes in Brittany to bouillabaisse in Marseille, encouraging expatriates to savor the unique flavors of each region.

- Farmers' Markets: Recommends visiting local farmers' markcts, where expatriates can purchase fresh produce, artisanal cheeses, and delectable pastries while engaging with local vendors.

- Wine and Gastronomy Tours: Highlights the opportunity to indulge in wine and gastronomy tours in renowned wine regions like Bordeaux and Burgundy, where expatriates can sample world-class wines and gourmet cuisine.

Section 3: Outdoor Pursuits

- Hiking and Cycling: Explores the vast network of hiking trails in the French countryside, such as the GR20 in Corsica and the Mont Blanc Circuit, offering breathtaking views and outdoor adventures.

- Skiing and Snowboarding: Discusses the renowned ski resorts in the French Alps, like Chamonix and Courchevel, providing expatriates with access to world-class winter sports and stunning alpine landscapes.

- Beaches and Water Activities: Highlights the beautiful beaches along the French Riviera and Atlantic coast, where expatriates can enjoy swimming, sailing, and water sports in the Mediterranean Sea and the Atlantic Ocean.

Section 4: Music, Festivals, and Entertainment

- Music Festivals: Explores the vibrant music scene in France, with festivals like Rock en Seine in Paris and Festival d'Avignon, showcasing a diverse range of musical performances.

- Cultural Festivals: Discusses cultural festivals like Carnaval de Nice and Fête de la Musique, which celebrate the country's traditions, arts, and music, providing expatriates with a taste of French culture.

- Theatres and Performances: Highlights the opportunity to attend theatrical productions, ballet performances, and opera shows in renowned venues like the Opéra Garnier in Paris.

In conclusion, Chapter 9 celebrates the abundance of cultural and leisure activities available to expatriates in France. Embracing the country's art, history, cuisine, and outdoor pursuits allows expatriates to fully immerse themselves in French culture and lifestyle. From exploring world-class museums and landmarks to indulging in culinary delights and outdoor adventures, expatriates can savor the diverse and captivating offerings of this culturally rich and picturesque country. By participating in local festivals, attending performances, and engaging in leisure activities, expatriates can foster a deep appreciation for the essence of French life while creating cherished memories of their time in France.

1. Art and History

Section 1 of this guide explores the captivating world of art and history in France, offering expatriates a wealth of cultural experiences that showcase the country's rich heritage and artistic contributions to the world.

France is renowned for its exceptional art museums and galleries, making it a paradise for art enthusiasts. The Louvre, located in Paris, is one of the world's largest and most famous museums, housing an impressive collection of art spanning thousands of years, including iconic masterpieces like the Mona Lisa and the Venus de Milo. The Musée d'Orsay is another must-visit museum, specializing in impressionist and post-impressionist art, featuring works by Van Gogh, Monet, Renoir, and more. The Centre Pompidou, known for its distinctive architectural design, focuses on modern and contemporary art, showcasing pieces by artists like Picasso, Duchamp, and Kandinsky.

Beyond the capital, France is dotted with regional museums that provide insight into local history and culture. From the Musée des Beaux-Arts in Lyon to the Musée des Augustins in Toulouse, these museums offer a glimpse into the unique artistry and heritage of different regions.

France's history is intricately woven into its architectural treasures and historic landmarks. The Eiffel Tower, an iconic symbol of the country, stands tall as a testament to France's engineering prowess and serves as a magnificent backdrop to the city of Paris. The Notre-Dame Cathedral, with its awe-inspiring Gothic architecture, is a magnificent religious and cultural monument that has stood the test of time.

For history enthusiasts, France boasts an array of châteaux and palaces that transport visitors to different eras. The opulent Palace of Versailles, once the residence of French kings, is a UNESCO World Heritage Site and a masterpiece of baroque architecture. The Loire Valley is dotted with fairytale-like châteaux, including Château de Chambord and Château de Chenonceau, showcasing the grandeur and splendor of French history.

Visiting these cultural landmarks allows expatriates to immerse themselves in the country's artistic and historical legacy, deepening their understanding of France's past and present. Whether exploring world-class art museums, marveling at architectural wonders, or stepping back in time through historic palaces and châteaux, expatriates have endless opportunities to embrace the cultural richness and artistic treasures that define France's unique identity. Engaging with the art and history of France is not only an educational experience but also a profound way for expatriates to connect with the country and develop a profound appreciation for its remarkable cultural contributions to the world.

2. Culinary Delights

Section 2 of this guide indulges in the culinary wonders of France, presenting expatriates with a gastronomic journey through the country's diverse and delectable cuisine.

France is celebrated worldwide for its culinary excellence and is rightfully considered a paradise for food enthusiasts. Each region boasts its own unique specialties, making the country a tapestry of flavors and tastes.

Local cuisine plays a central role in French culture, and expatriates have the opportunity to savor a vast array of dishes. In Brittany, expatriates can relish savory and sweet crêpes, while in the south of France, they can delight in bouillabaisse, a traditional fisherman's stew bursting with Mediterranean flavors. The Alsace region offers the iconic tarte flambée, a thin crust pizza-like dish with toppings of cream, onions, and bacon, while Burgundy entices with its coq au vin, a succulent chicken dish braised in red wine.

For expatriates looking to experience authentic French cuisine, visiting farmers' markets is a must. These vibrant markets are abundant with fresh produce, artisanal cheeses, and delectable pastries. Engaging with local vendors offers a delightful cultural exchange, allowing expatriates to discover the seasonal delights of France and support local farmers and producers.

France's reputation for world-class wines and gastronomy is well-deserved, and expatriates can partake in wine and gastronomy tours to explore the country's famous wine regions. Bordeaux, renowned for its red wines, offers picturesque vineyards and wine-tasting experiences, while Burgundy's prestigious vineyards produce exceptional white wines. Alongside the wine, French gastronomy celebrates a rich tapestry of flavors, and attending a Michelin-starred restaurant or savoring traditional meals at a local bistro provides expatriates with an unforgettable dining experience.

French cuisine extends beyond formal dining, with street food and culinary festivals adding to the culinary adventure. From indulging in buttery croissants for breakfast to savoring flaky pain au chocolat as an afternoon treat, expatriates can embrace the art of French patisserie. Local markets and festivals offer opportunities to try regional specialties like socca in Nice, cassoulet in Toulouse, and escargot in Burgundy.

For expatriates with a passion for cooking, taking culinary classes in France can be an enriching experience. Learning the art of French cuisine from experienced chefs not only imparts culinary skills but also provides a deeper understanding of the cultural significance of food in French society.

In conclusion, Section 2 celebrates the culinary delights of France, offering expatriates a feast for the senses and a profound exploration of the country's rich food culture. From savoring regional specialties at local markets to indulging in the finest dining experiences, expatriates have the privilege to partake in France's culinary legacy. Embracing French cuisine allows expatriates to connect with the heart of the culture, fostering a deeper appreciation for the country's traditions and culinary excellence. By relishing the flavors of France, expatriates can create cherished memories and a profound understanding of the role food plays in shaping the country's unique identity.

3. Outdoor Pursuits

Section 3 of this guide invites expatriates in France to explore the country's diverse outdoor pursuits, offering a wide array of activities that take advantage of the country's breathtaking landscapes and natural wonders.

France's countryside is a paradise for hikers and nature enthusiasts. The country boasts an extensive network of hiking trails that wind through picturesque landscapes, from the rugged cliffs of Brittany to the serene hills of Provence. The GR20 in Corsica is renowned as one of the most challenging and beautiful long-distance hiking trails in Europe, offering breathtaking views of mountain peaks, crystal-clear lakes, and lush forests.

Cycling is another popular outdoor activity in France, with countless cycling routes catering to both leisurely riders and avid cyclists. The Loire Valley, known for its stunning châteaux, offers scenic cycling paths that wind through vineyards and historic villages. Cycling along the banks of the Canal du Midi in the south of France provides a leisurely way to explore the tranquil beauty of the region.

During the winter months, France's majestic Alps become a playground for skiers and snowboarders. World-class ski resorts like Chamonix, Courchevel, and Val d'Isère offer exhilarating slopes and powder-covered peaks, attracting winter sports enthusiasts from around the globe. Beyond skiing, the Alps also offer opportunities for snowshoeing, ice climbing, and snowmobiling, making it a winter wonderland for outdoor adventurers.

France's diverse coastline provides ample opportunities for beach lovers and water enthusiasts. The French Riviera is famed for its glamorous beaches, where expatriates can soak up the Mediterranean sun and enjoy the vibrant coastal atmosphere. The Atlantic coast, on the other hand, is a haven for surfers, with renowned surf spots in Biarritz and Hossegor attracting wave riders from all over the world.

For those seeking a more tranquil outdoor experience, France's countryside offers idyllic settings for picnics, birdwatching, and stargazing. The Gorges du Verdon, often called the "Grand Canyon of Europe," provides stunning natural scenery for hiking and boating, while the lavender fields of Provence create a dreamlike landscape that captivates the senses.

France's diverse outdoor pursuits offer something for everyone, from adrenaline junkies to nature lovers and those seeking relaxation and tranquility. Engaging in outdoor activities not only allows expatriates to explore the country's natural beauty but also provides an opportunity to connect with like-minded individuals who share a love for adventure and the great outdoors.

In conclusion, Section 3 celebrates the diverse outdoor pursuits that France has to offer, providing expatriates with a plethora of activities to enjoy throughout the year. From hiking and cycling in stunning landscapes to skiing in the majestic Alps and basking in the sun on beautiful beaches, France's outdoor opportunities cater to all interests and preferences. By immersing themselves in outdoor adventures, expatriates can create cherished memories and develop a profound appreciation for the country's natural treasures. Embracing the outdoors in France is a gateway to discovering the country's splendor, fostering a deep connection with the land and its people, and making the most of the extraordinary expatriate experience in this breathtakingly beautiful country.

4. Music, Festivals, and Entertainment

Section 4 of this guide delves into the vibrant world of music, festivals, and entertainment in France, presenting expatriates with a myriad of cultural experiences and opportunities for entertainment that celebrate the country's artistic spirit and joie de vivre.

France's music scene is as diverse as its cultural heritage, offering a wide range of genres and performances to suit every taste. From classical music to contemporary pop, jazz, and electronic music, expatriates can indulge in concerts and live performances across the country. Paris, as the cultural capital, hosts numerous renowned venues such as the Opéra Garnier and the Philharmonie de Paris, where world-class musicians and orchestras showcase their talents.

The country's festival calendar is brimming with cultural events that celebrate French traditions and international artistry. The Festival d'Avignon, held annually in the historic city of Avignon, is one of the world's most significant performing arts festivals, attracting theater enthusiasts and artists from around the globe. The Cannes Film Festival, renowned for its glamorous red carpet events and premieres, showcases the best of international cinema, offering expatriates a taste of the glitz and glamour of the film industry.

Music festivals in France are also a highlight, drawing crowds of music lovers to revel in the spirit of live performances. Rock en Seine in Paris, Vieilles Charrues in Brittany, and Eurockéennes de Belfort in eastern France are just a few of the major music festivals that bring together artists from various genres and nationalities, creating a vibrant atmosphere of shared enthusiasm and celebration.

Cultural festivals offer an insight into the traditions and customs that shape France's regional identity. The Carnaval de Nice, with its dazzling parades and floats, transforms the city into a colorful spectacle, while the Fête de la Musique on June 21st marks the summer solstice with free music performances on the streets, squares, and parks across the country.

In addition to festivals, France's entertainment scene encompasses theater, ballet, opera, and comedy. The Théâtre du Châtelet and Opéra Bastille in Paris present world-class productions, while regional theaters across the country showcase performances that celebrate the French theatrical tradition.

France's love for cinema is evident in its many film festivals and the extensive network of cinemas screening a wide variety of films, from mainstream blockbusters to independent and art-house cinema. The French appreciation for cinema and storytelling contributes to the country's prominent role in the global film industry.

In conclusion, Section 4 celebrates the vibrant world of music, festivals, and entertainment in France, offering expatriates an abundance of cultural experiences and opportunities for enjoyment. From attending classical concerts at iconic venues to dancing at music festivals, expatriates have a plethora of options to indulge in the country's artistic and festive spirit. Engaging in cultural festivals and entertainment events not only allows expatriates to celebrate France's creative essence but also provides a platform for connecting with locals and fellow expatriates who share a passion for culture and the arts. By immersing themselves in the music, festivals, and entertainment scene, expatriates can enrich their experience in France and create lasting memories of the country's dynamic and diverse cultural landscape.

Chapter 10: Overcoming Challenges and Celebrating Success

Chapter 10 of this guide acknowledges the inevitable challenges expatriates may encounter while living in France and offers insights on how to overcome them. It also emphasizes the importance of celebrating successes, both big and small, throughout the expatriate journey.

Section 1: Overcoming Challenges

- Language Barrier: Addresses the potential language barrier expatriates may face, providing tips on language learning resources, language exchange opportunities, and the value of persistence in improving language skills.

- Cultural Adjustment: Explores the process of adapting to a new culture, discussing the stages of culture shock and suggesting ways to embrace cultural differences with an open mind and a willingness to learn.

- Bureaucratic Procedures: Offers guidance on navigating the bureaucratic procedures involved in obtaining residency permits, healthcare registration, and other administrative tasks, emphasizing the importance of seeking assistance when needed.

- Building a Support Network: Emphasizes the significance of building a support network of friends, expatriate groups, and local communities to combat feelings of isolation and loneliness.

- Homesickness: Acknowledges the reality of homesickness and provides coping strategies, such as staying connected with loved ones, engaging in familiar activities, and exploring new hobbies to create a sense of comfort in the new environment.

Section 2: Celebrating Success

- Small Achievements: Encourages expatriates to celebrate small achievements, such as successfully navigating public transportation or having a meaningful conversation in the local language, as these milestones contribute to personal growth and confidence.

- Cultural Milestones: Recognizes the importance of embracing and participating in cultural celebrations and milestones, such as local festivals and traditions, as a way to immerse oneself in the local culture and create lasting memories.

- Professional Accomplishments: Highlights the value of acknowledging professional accomplishments and milestones, whether in a job, entrepreneurial endeavor, or personal project, to foster a sense of achievement and motivation.

- Personal Growth: Reflects on the personal growth and resilience gained from overcoming challenges and adapting to a new environment, encouraging expatriates to recognize and appreciate their own growth throughout the journey.

- Embracing Multicultural Experiences: Celebrates the richness of multicultural experiences in France and the opportunity to connect with people from diverse backgrounds, fostering a sense of global citizenship and appreciation for cultural diversity.

In conclusion, Chapter 10 addresses the challenges expatriates may face while living in France and empowers them to overcome these hurdles with determination and adaptability. By embracing the process of cultural adjustment, building a support network, and seeking assistance when needed, expatriates can transform challenges into opportunities for personal and cultural growth. Moreover, the chapter emphasizes the significance of celebrating successes, no matter how small, and appreciating the milestones achieved throughout the expatriate journey. By acknowledging personal achievements, embracing cultural experiences, and cultivating a positive mindset, expatriates can create a fulfilling and enriching experience while living in this vibrant and welcoming country.

1. Overcoming Challenges

Section 1 of this guide delves into the various challenges expatriates may encounter while living in France and offers practical strategies to overcome them, enabling a smoother and more fulfilling expatriate experience.

One of the primary challenges for expatriates in France is the language barrier. While English is commonly spoken in urban areas and tourist destinations, embracing the local language, French, is essential for deeper integration into the culture. Expatriates can overcome this challenge by enrolling in language classes, using language learning apps, and engaging in language exchange programs with native speakers. Embracing every opportunity to practice speaking French, even if it feels uncomfortable at first, will lead to greater confidence and ease in communication with locals.

Another aspect of the expatriate journey is cultural adjustment. Moving to a new country with different customs, traditions, and social norms can be overwhelming. Expatriates may experience culture shock, a process involving different stages of emotional response to the unfamiliar environment. To overcome culture shock, it is crucial to approach cultural differences with an open mind and a willingness to learn. Engaging in local customs and traditions, attending cultural events, and making an effort to understand the values and beliefs of the French society can facilitate a smoother adjustment.

Navigating bureaucratic procedures can be another challenge for expatriates. Acquiring a residence permit, opening a bank account, or accessing healthcare services may involve complex paperwork and unfamiliar processes. Seeking assistance from relocation services, expatriate support organizations, or local authorities can help simplify the bureaucratic journey and ensure compliance with legal requirements.

Building a support network is essential for expatriates, especially those who are far away from their original support systems. Feeling isolated and homesick is a common challenge, but connecting with other expatriates, joining local clubs or interest groups, and participating in community events can help create a sense of belonging and companionship. Establishing meaningful friendships with both locals and fellow expatriates can enrich the expatriate experience and provide a reliable support system during challenging times.

Homesickness is yet another hurdle faced by expatriates. To cope with homesickness, staying connected with loved ones back home through regular communication, video calls, and social media can provide comfort and a sense of familiarity. Additionally, exploring new hobbies, participating in local activities, and immersing oneself in the cultural richness of France can create a sense of home and belonging in the new environment.

In conclusion, Section 1 acknowledges the challenges expatriates may encounter while living in France and provides valuable strategies to overcome them. By proactively tackling the language barrier, embracing cultural differences, seeking assistance with administrative processes, building a support network, and finding ways to cope with homesickness, expatriates can navigate the expatriate journey with resilience and adaptability. Each challenge presents an opportunity for personal growth and cultural enrichment, enabling expatriates to embrace the beauty and diversity of France while creating a meaningful and rewarding experience in their new home.

2. Celebrating Success

Section 2 of this guide celebrates the importance of recognizing and celebrating success during the expatriate journey in France. From small achievements to significant milestones, acknowledging and embracing moments of success can enhance the expatriate experience and foster a positive outlook on the overall adventure.

Celebrating small achievements is a key aspect of the expatriate experience. Learning a few basic phrases in French, successfully navigating the local public transportation system, or making a new friend from a different cultural background are all examples of small victories that deserve recognition. By acknowledging these accomplishments, expatriates can build self-confidence and motivation, empowering them to continue exploring and adapting to their new environment.

Cultural milestones offer unique opportunities for celebration and participation in the rich tapestry of French traditions and festivities. Engaging in local festivals, such as Bastille Day on July 14th, witnessing the dazzling displays of fireworks, and partaking in festive parades, can create lasting memories and deepen the connection with French culture. Embracing cultural milestones allows expatriates to forge meaningful bonds with locals, fostering a sense of belonging and acceptance within the community.

Recognizing professional accomplishments is equally vital for expatriates. Whether succeeding in a new job, launching a business, or achieving personal career goals, acknowledging these achievements can fuel ambition and inspire further growth. Celebrating professional milestones reinforces the sense of achievement and dedication in pursuing career aspirations while adapting to the professional landscape in France.

Beyond the professional sphere, personal growth is a cause for celebration. Overcoming challenges, such as mastering the local language or adapting to cultural norms, represents significant personal growth and resilience. Expatriates can take pride in their adaptability, open-mindedness, and willingness to learn, recognizing these qualities as invaluable assets in navigating the complexities of living abroad.

Embracing multicultural experiences is yet another reason to celebrate. Engaging with people from diverse backgrounds fosters an understanding of global citizenship and appreciation for cultural diversity. Expatriates can cherish the enriching friendships and connections they forge with individuals from different parts of the world, contributing to a more inclusive and compassionate worldview.

In conclusion, Section 2 highlights the importance of celebrating success during the expatriate journey in France. By recognizing and embracing small achievements, engaging in local traditions, celebrating professional accomplishments, acknowledging personal growth, and valuing multicultural experiences, expatriates can cultivate a sense of fulfillment and joy throughout their time in France. Celebrating success not only enhances the overall expatriate experience but also contributes to a positive and optimistic outlook, enriching the journey of cultural exploration and personal development in this enchanting and diverse country.

Appendix: Useful Resources and Contacts

This appendix provides a comprehensive list of useful resources and contacts for expatriates living in France. These resources offer assistance and support across various aspects of expatriate life, including administrative procedures, language learning, cultural integration, healthcare, and more.

1. Language Learning:

- Alliance Française: A renowned language school with branches across France, offering French language courses for all levels.

- Duolingo: A popular language-learning app with a user-friendly interface, providing interactive French language lessons.

- Tandem Language Exchange: An online platform connecting language learners for language exchange sessions with native speakers.

2. Administrative Support:

- Service-Public.fr: The official French government website providing information and guidance on administrative procedures.

- Expat.com: An expatriate community platform offering valuable advice and resources for those living in France.

- Your Local Mairie (Town Hall): Local town halls are excellent resources for information on residency permits, voter registration, and other administrative matters.

3. Healthcare and Insurance:

- Assurance Maladie (French Health Insurance): The official French healthcare website, offering information on health coverage and registration.

- Private Health Insurance Providers: Companies like AXA, Bupa, and Cigna offer private health insurance plans for expatriates.

- SOS Médecins: An emergency medical service providing house calls and medical assistance 24/7.

4. Housing and Accommodation:

- Leboncoin.fr: A popular online platform for finding rental properties and buying/selling items.

- Airbnb: Useful for short-term accommodation options while searching for a more permanent home.

- Real Estate Agencies: Local real estate agencies can assist with finding suitable rental or purchase properties.

5. Expat Communities and Support:

- InterNations: A global expatriate community with local groups and events in major cities in France.

- Expatica France: An online resource providing articles, forums, and events for expatriates in France.

- Meetup: An app and website hosting various social and interest-based groups, including expat meetups.

6. Legal and Financial Advice:

- Expat Legal Services: Law firms specializing in expatriate legal matters, including visa and residence permit applications.

- Tax Advisors: Seeking advice from tax professionals experienced in expatriate taxation can be beneficial.

7. Transportation:

- SNCF: France's national railway company, offering train services connecting major cities and regions.

- RATP: The public transportation authority in Paris, providing information on metro, bus, and tram services in the capital.

8. Emergency Services:

- Police: For emergencies and reporting crimes, call 17.

- Fire Department: For emergencies related to fires and accidents, call 18.

- Medical Emergencies: For urgent medical assistance, call 15.

This comprehensive list of resources and contacts serves as a valuable guide for expatriates navigating life in France. Whether seeking language learning opportunities, administrative support, healthcare information, housing options, or connecting with expat communities, these resources are designed to support expatriates in their journey of cultural exploration and successful integration into French society.

Printed in Great Britain
by Amazon

38909786R00063